"This Is My Body"

"This Is My Body"

Eucharistic Reflections Inspired by
Adoro Te Devote *and* Ave Verum

Raniero Cantalamessa

Pauline
BOOKS & MEDIA
Boston

Library of Congress Cataloging-in-Publication Data

Cantalamessa, Raniero.
  [Meditations. English. Selections]
  This is my body : eucharistic reflections inspired by Adoro Te Devote and Ave Verum / Raniero Cantalamessa.
    p. cm.
  ISBN 0-8198-7415-9 (pbk.)
  1. Lord's Supper—Catholic Church—Sermons. 2. Hymns, Latin—History and criticism. 3. Catholic Church—Sermons. 4. Sermons, Italian—Translations into English. I. Title.
  BX2215.3.C36 2005
  252'.02—dc22

                              2005009827

The Scripture quotations contained herein are from the Catholic Edition of the Revised Standard Version of the Bible, copyright 1965, 1966 by the Division of Christian Education of the National Council of the Churches of Christ in the United States of America. Used by permission. All rights reserved.

Cover art: Bouts, Dieric the Elder (c. 1415–1475). The Lord's Supper. Erich Lessing / Art Resource, NY

"P" and PAULINE are registered trademarks of the Daughters of St. Paul.

Copyright © 2005, P. Raniero Cantalamessa

Published by Pauline Books & Media, 50 Saint Pauls Avenue, Boston, MA 02130-3491.

Printed in U.S.A.

www.pauline.org

Pauline Books & Media is the publishing house of the Daughters of St. Paul, an international congregation of women religious serving the Church with the communications media.

1 2 3 4 5 6 7 8 9   11 10 09 08 07 06 05

Contents

To the Reverend Father Raniero Cantalamessa, O.F.M. CAP.
Preacher to the Pontifical Household

Today's meeting concludes the cycle of Lenten sermons, during which you have completed the series of meditations on the hymn *Adoro Te Devote,* which began in Advent.

This year, contemplation of the Eucharist accompanies the whole Church on an exacting journey of profound study of the many aspects of this incomparable Sacrament, source and summit of her life and mission in the world.

From my heart I thank you for the abundance of points you put forward for meditation, and for the spirit-filled way in which you presented them.

I assure you of my constant remembrance in prayer, so that your ministry may be always fruitful. As Easter approaches, I send you my heartfelt good wishes, accompanied by a special Apostolic Blessing, which I extend to all those whom you meet in your daily service to the Church.

From the Vatican
March 18, 2005

Joannes Paulus PP. II

Introduction

This book is a collection of meditations on the Eucharist that I gave at the Pontifical Household during Advent and Lent in the Year of the Eucharist 2004–2005. The first Eucharistic Year, proclaimed by John Paul II in 1985, offered me the occasion to write the series of meditations titled "The Eucharist, Our Sanctification"; this second Eucharistic Year has given me the opportunity to offer this new series of meditations based on a commentary on two of the most well-known and venerated Eucharistic hymns of the Latin Church: the *Adoro Te Devote* and the *Ave Verum.*

They are the last meditations that I had the honor and grace to be able to hold in the presence of the Holy Father John Paul II. During the sermons preached in Lent 2005, he was repeatedly hospitalized in conditions of health that the whole world followed with trepidation, and that ended with his holy death. And yet, even in these conditions he wished to follow, through a special television connection, the reflections of a simple priest of his Church, giving to all, and above all the preacher, an example of humility and of extraordinary love of the Eucharist. I consider the letter that the Holy Father wrote me, at the conclusion of the cycle of meditations, the best recompense for my twenty-five years of service as Pontifical Household preacher.

In a poem written in his youth, Karol Wojtyła praised the vocation of being a "Eucharistic I"; as pope he realized this calling before the Church and the world. In the penultimate chapter of this book there is a description of the edifying death of a great lover of the Eucharist, St. Thomas Aquinas. John Paul II's death was no different. It is comforting to think that for him what is written in the last stanza of the *Adoro Te Devote* is now a reality:

Jesus! Whom for the present veil'd I see,
what I so thirst for, O vouchsafe to me:
that I may see Thy countenance unfolding,
and may be blest Thy glory in beholding.

Adoro Te Devote

Adóro te devóte, latens Déitas,
quae sub his figúris vere látitas:
tibi se cor meum totum súbicit,
quia te contémplans totum déficit.

Visus, tactus, gustus in te fállitur,
sed audítu solo tuto créditur.
Credo quidquid dixit Dei Fílius;
nil hoc verbo veritátis vérius.

In cruce latébat sola déitas;
at hic latet simul et humánitas.
Ambo tamen credens atque cónfitens
peto quod petívit latro poénitens.

Plagas sicut Thomas non intúeor;
Deum tamen meum te confíteor.
Fac me tibi semper magis crédere,
in te spem habére, te dilígere.

O memoriále mortis Dómini,
Panis vivus vitam praestans hómini,
praesta meae menti de te vívere,
et te illi semper dulce sápere.

Pie Pellicánae, Jesu Dómine,
me immúndum munda tuo sánguine,
cujus una stilla salvum fácere
totum mundum quit ab omni scélere.

Jesu quem velátum nunc auspício,
oro fiat illud quod tam sítio:
ut, te reveláta cernens fácie,
visu sim beátus tuae glóriae. Amen.

Adoro Te Devote

O Godhead hid, devoutly I adore Thee,
who truly art within the forms before me;
to Thee my heart I bow with bended knee,
as failing quite in contemplating Thee.

Sight, touch, and taste in Thee are each deceived;
the ear alone most safely is believed:
I believe all the Son of God has spoken,
than Truth's own word there is no truer token.

God only on the cross lay hid from view;
but here lies hid at once the Manhood too;
and I, in both professing my belief,
make the same prayer as the repentant thief.

Thy wounds, as Thomas saw, I do not see;
yet Thee confess my Lord and God to be:
make me believe Thee ever more and more;
in Thee my hope, in Thee my love to store.

O thou Memorial of our Lord's own dying!
O Bread that living art and vivifying!
Make ever Thou my soul on Thee to live;
ever a taste of Heavenly sweetness give.

O loving Pelican! O Jesus Lord!
Unclean I am, but cleanse me in Thy blood;
of which a single drop, for sinners spilt,
is ransom for a world's entire guilt.

Jesus! Whom for the present veil'd I see,
what I so thirst for, O vouchsafe to me:
That I may see Thy countenance unfolding,
and may be blest Thy glory in beholding. Amen.

Translated by E. Caswall (1814–1878)

I.

Everything Fails in Contemplating Thee

Eucharistic Adoration

The *Adoro Te Devote* has been described as "a harmonious and brilliant composition, very rich and simple, that has served, more than so many books, to form Catholic Eucharistic piety."[1] The history of the hymn is quite singular. It is commonly attributed to St. Thomas Aquinas, but the first testimonies of such an attribution date back no less than fifty years after his death, which occurred in 1274. A recently discovered addition, on the margin of a late manuscript of the life of St. Thomas, makes the *Adoro Te Devote* the prayer which the saint recited when receiving Viaticum at the point of death.[2] But

---

1. A. Wilmart, *La tradition littéraire et textuelle de "l'Adoro te devote,"* in *Recherches de Théologie ancienne et médiévale,* 1, 1929, p. 21.

2. Cf. Guilelmus de Tocco, *Ystoria sancti Thomae de Aquino,* ed. C. le Brun-Gouanvic, Pontifical Institute of Mediaeval Studies (Toronto, 1996), p. 197. I do not think the reasons in favor of the authenticity of the other additions in the manuscript (pp. 72–76) can be applied to the addition containing the *Adoro Te Devote,* this one being public knowledge at the time the manuscript was composed.

it seems rather unlikely that under such circumstances he would have been able to improvise such a theologically and poetically elaborate text. In any event, if the literary paternity is destined to remain uncertain (as is the case of the other Eucharistic hymns that are attributed to Aquinas), undoubtedly the hymn is in the vein of his thought and spirituality.

The text remained all but unknown for two more centuries and perhaps it would have continued to be so if St. Pius V had not inserted it among the prayers of preparation and thanksgiving for the Mass printed in the Missal reformed by him in 1570. From that date, the hymn was used in the universal Church as one of the most loved Eucharistic prayers of the clergy and the Christian people. It would be a grave loss if the abandonment of Latin ended by relegating this hymn to the oblivion from which St. Pius V rescued it. There are metrical versions of it in the principal languages, which can be sung with the same Gregorian melody of the Latin. One version, in English, is the work of the great Jesuit poet, Gerard Manley Hopkins.

To pray with the words of the *Adoro Te Devote* means to allow ourselves to be carried by the warm wave of Eucharistic piety of the generations that preceded us, of the many saints that sang it. It means, perhaps, to relive emotions and memories that we ourselves experienced when singing it in certain grace-filled moments of our lives. This, however, is not a book on the *Adoro Te Devote*, but on the Eucharist! The hymn is only a map that helps us to explore the territory, the guide that explains the work of art.

1. A Hidden Presence

In this meditation we reflect on the first stanza of the hymn, which in the most popular rhythmic version reads as follows:

Adóro devóte, latens Déitas,
te quae sub his formis vere látitas:
tibi se cor meum totum súbicit,
quia te contémplans totum déficit.

O Godhead hid, devoutly I adore Thee,
who truly art within the forms before me;
to Thee my heart I bow with bended knee,
as failing quite in contemplating Thee.

Attempts were made to establish the critical text of the hymn based on a few manuscripts existing prior to printing.[3] The variations we know in regard to the text are not many. The principal one refers precisely to the first two verses of this stanza, which would have read like this: *Adoro devote latens veritas / Te qui sub his formis vere latitas,* "O hidden Truth, devoutly I adore Thee, who truly art within these forms concealed." *"Veritas"* would obviously stand for the person of Christ, and *"formis"* would be the equivalent of *"figures,"* that is, the Eucharistic species.

---

3. A. Wilmart, *La tradition littéraire*, pp. 21–40, 149–176. The text established by Wilmart was inserted in the Roman Ritual promulgated after the liturgical reform of Vatican II: cf. *De sacra comunione et de cultu mysterii eucharistici extra Missam* (Libreria Vaticana, 1973, p. 61ff.). The first fourteen lines of the hymn all end with a consonant, while the remaining fourteen end with a vowel; neither the style nor the content however seem to imply the will of the author to divide the text into two parts.

Displacing the pronoun "Thee" to the second verse seems necessary inasmuch as keeping it in the first verse *(Adoro te devote)* would make it one syllable longer than the others. Consequently, one must accept, for rhythmical reasons, the word *formis* instead of *figuris.* Less convincing is the correction of *latens deitas* (hidden Godhead) to *latens veritas* (hidden Truth). In favor of *"latens Deitas"* is the parallelism with *"latens humanitas"* (hidden humanity) of the third stanza and also the possible allusion to Isaiah 45:15: *"Vere tu es Deus absconditus"* ("Truly thou art a hidden God"). If that was not the original lection, it is true, nevertheless, that the one who introduced it improved and did not worsen the text, and the current use does well to keep it.

The *Adoro Te Devote,* as other venerated Latin liturgical hymns of the past, belongs to the collectivity of the faithful, who sang it for centuries and made it their own no less than the author who composed it. The published text does not for this reason have less value and authority than the critical text and it is with it, in fact, that the hymn continues to be known and sung in the whole Church.

In every stanza of the *Adoro Te Devote* there is a theological affirmation and an invocation, which is the prayerful answer of the soul to the mystery. In the first stanza the theological truth evoked refers to the mode of the presence of Christ in the Eucharistic species. The Latin expression *"vere latitas"* is full of meaning. It means: you are hidden, but you are really there (where the accent is on *"vere,"* on the reality of the presence); and it also means: you are really there but hidden (with the accent on *"latitas,"* on the sacramental character of this presence, mediated by signs).

To understand this way of speaking of the Eucharist it is necessary to keep in mind the "great change" that takes place regarding the Eucharist in the passage of the symbolic theology of the Fathers and the dialectic of Scholasticism. The change had its remote beginnings in the ninth century with Paschasius Radbertus and Ratramnus of Corbie: the first a defender of a physical and material presence of Christ in the bread and wine; the second a defender of a true and real presence, but sacramental, not physical. It burst forth openly, however, only two centuries later, with Berengarius of Tours (c. 1088), who accentuated the symbolic and sacramental character of Christ in the Eucharist to such a point as to jeopardize faith in the objective reality of such a presence.

While at first it was said that Christ is present sacramentally in the Eucharist, now, with a language borrowed from Aristotle, it is said that he is present substantially, or according to substance. *Figura,* or *forma,* no longer indicates, as *sacramentum,* the ensemble of signs with which the presence of Christ is realized, but simply the "species or appearances" of bread and wine—in technical language, the accidents.[4]

Our hymn is placed clearly on this side of the change, even if it avoids recourse to new philosophical terms, not very appropriate in a poetic text. The word "figure," or "form," indicates the species of bread and wine inasmuch

---

4. Cf. Henri de Lubac, *Corpus mysticum: L'Eucharistie et l'Eglise dans le Moyen Age* (Paris: Aubier, 1949), p. 252.

as they conceal what they contain and contain what they conceal.[5]

But it is not just about simple theological specifications. With its insistence on the concealment of the divinity in the species of bread and wine *(latens* deitas, vere *latitas,* Jesum quem *velatum)* the author evokes, as mentioned, the biblical topic of the *Deus absconditus* (Is 45:15), of the God who reveals himself by concealing himself. The veil, in creation, is constituted by things; in the Bible, it consists of words; in the Incarnation, it consists of the humanity of Christ; in the Eucharist, it is constituted by the species of bread and wine. St. Alphonsus Mary de Liguori, in a clear reference to the words of our hymn, writes:

> *Truly you are a hidden God* (Is 45:15). In no other work of divine love do these words prove so true as in the adorable mystery of the most holy Eucharist, where our God is completely hidden. In taking flesh, the Eternal Word hid his divinity and appeared as a man on the earth; but in abiding with us in this sacrament, Jesus hides his humanity too, and, as St. Bernard says, only appears as bread in order to demonstrate thereby the tender love he has for us. The divinity is hidden, the humanity is hidden, only the depths of love are manifest. *(Latet divinitas, latet humanitas, sola patent viscera caritatis).*[6]

---

5. Cf. St. Thomas Aquinas, *On the Gospel of John,* VI, lectio 6, no. 954: "The manna only prefigured, while this bread contains that which it represents" *(continet quod figurat).*

6. St. Alphonsus M. de Liguori, *Visits to the Blessed Sacrament,* XXIV, in *Opere ascetiche,* IV (Rome, 1939), p. 365. Only the last part of the sentence quoted goes back to St. Bernard *(Serm. in Cant.* 61, 4: *patent viscera misericordiae),* the rest belongs to the *Adoro Te Devote.*

The Fathers expressed this same intuition with the concept of divine condescension, the *synkatabasis*. St. Francis speaks more explicitly, in both cases, of the humility of God: "Behold, each day he humbles himself as when he came from the royal throne into the Virgin's womb; each day he himself comes to us, appearing humbly; each day he comes down from the bosom of the Father upon the altar in the hands of a priest." "O sublime humility! O humble sublimity! The Lord of the universe, God and the Son of God, so humbles himself that for our salvation he hides himself under an ordinary piece of bread!"[7]

2. In Devout Adoration

I mentioned that in every stanza of the hymn we find a theological affirmation followed by an invocation with which the one praying responds to it and appropriates the truth evoked. To the affirmation of the real presence, even if hidden, of Christ in the bread and the wine, the author responds, melting literally in devout adoration and bringing with him, in the same movement, the innumerable souls that for more than half a millennium have prayed with his words. The first stanza of the *Adoro Te Devote* is "brimming with adoration."[8]

"Adoro": this word that opens the hymn is on its own a profession of faith in the identity between the

---

7. St. Francis of Assisi, *The Admonition*, I, and *Letter to the Entire Order* (*Early Documents*, I, New York, 1999, pp. 118 and 129). On the contribution of St. Francis to the Eucharistic renewal of the thirteenth c., cf. B. Cornet, *Le "De reverentia corporis Christi." Exhortations et lettres de Saint François*, in *Etudes Franciscaines*, 58, 1956, pp. 155–171.

8. H. Clerissac, *L'Esprit de St. Dominique*, Ed. de la Vie spirituelle, St. Maximin, 1924, p. 182.

Eucharistic body and the historical body of Christ, "born of the Virgin Mary, and who really suffered and was immolated on the cross for man." It is only thanks to this identity, in fact, and to the hypostatic union in Christ between humanity and divinity, that we can be in adoration before the consecrated Host, without committing the sin of idolatry. St. Augustine already said: "In this flesh (the Lord) has walked here and this same flesh he has given us to eat for salvation; and no one eats that flesh without first having adored it.... We do not sin by adoring it, but rather we sin if we do not adore it."[9]

It was the New Testament that raised the word adoration (in Greek *proskynesis*) to a dignity until then unknown. In it, every time there is an attempt to adore anyone but God himself, the immediate reaction is: "Don't do it!" "It is God who must be adored."[10] Adoration, therefore, is the only religious act that cannot be offered to any other in the universe, not even to Our Lady, but only to God. Herein is its unique dignity and force. The same divine nature or consubstantiality of the Holy Spirit, before being expressed with these terms, was defined in the Creed of Constantinople, attributing to him the same adoration as to the Father: *simul adoratur.*

But, in what exactly does adoration consist and how is it manifested? Adoration may be prepared by long reflection, but it ends with an intuition, and, like every intuition, it does not last long. It is the perception of the grandeur, majesty, and beauty of God, together with his goodness and presence, which takes one's breath away. It

---

9. St. Augustine, *On the Psalms, 98:9* (PL 37, 1264).
10. Cf. Rev 19:10, 22:9; Acts 10:25–26, 14:13ff.

is a sort of sinking in the shoreless and fathomless ocean of God's majesty.

When adoration is genuine, it has nothing servile about it; it is not an expression of fear but of filial love and freedom. An expression of adoration, more effective than any word, is silence. To adore, according to the wonderful expression of St. Gregory of Nazianzus, means to raise a "hymn of silence" to God.[11] There was a time when, to enter into an atmosphere of adoration before the Most Blessed Sacrament, it was enough for me to repeat the first words of a hymn by the German Protestant mystic Gerhard Tersteegen:

> Lo, God is here! Let us adore,
> and own how dreadful is this place!
> Let all within us feel his power,
> and silent bow before his face;
> Who know his power, his grace who prove
> serve him with awe, with reverence love.[12]

Perhaps because the words of a foreign language are less worn-out by usage and trivialization, it is a fact that those words gave me, every time, an inner thrill. *"Gott ist gegenwartig!"* ("God is present, God is here!")—the words soon vanished, only the truth they had transmitted remained, the vivid feeling of the presence of God.

In our hymn, the meaning of adoration is reinforced by that of *devotion: "adoro te devote."* The Middle Ages gave this term a new meaning in relation to pagan and also Christian antiquity. At the beginning, it indicated the attachment of a person, expressed in faithful service and,

---

11. St. Gregory of Nazianzus, *Carmina*, 29 (PG 37, 507).

12. G. Tersteegen (d. 1769), *Geistliches Blumengärtlein* 11, (Stuttgart, 1969), p. 340ff. (translated by John Wesley).

in Christian usage, every form of divine service, especially the liturgical service of the recitation of the psalms and prayers.

In the great spiritual authors of the Middle Ages the word is interiorized, no longer signifying exterior practices, but the profound dispositions of the heart. For St. Bernard it indicates "the interior fervor of the soul burning with the fire of charity."[13] With St. Bonaventure and his school the person of Christ becomes the central object of devotion, understood as the feeling of overwhelming gratitude and love aroused by the memory of his benefits. The Angelic Doctor dedicates two whole articles of the *Summa* to devotion, which he considers the first and most important act of the virtue of religion.[14] For him it consists of the readiness and disposition of the will to offer itself to God, which is expressed in a service without reservations and full of fervor.

This rich and profound content was unfortunately lost to a great extent later on, when the concept of "devotion" was placed alongside that of "devotions," namely of exterior and special practices addressed not only to God, but also more often to saints or to particular places, motives, and images. To engage in one's own devotions meant to recite the prayers in use. There was a return in practice to the old meaning of the term.

In our hymn the adverb *devote* keeps intact the theological and spiritual force that the author himself (if it is St. Thomas Aquinas) had contributed. The best explanation of what is meant by *devotio* in our hymn is in the

13. Cf. J. Charillon, art. *Devotio,* in *Dict. Spir.,* 3, col. 711.

14. Aquinas, *S. Th.,* II, IIae, q. 82, a. 1–2; cf. J. W. Curran, art. *Dévotion, Fondement théologique,* in *Dict. Spir.,* III, col. 716ff.

words that follow in the second part of the stanza: *Tibi se cor meum totum subiicit* (to you my whole heart abandons itself), namely, total and loving readiness to do the will of God.

3. Eucharistic Contemplation

What remains is to be receptive of the highest blaze: "Everything fails in contemplating Thee" *(te contemplans totum deficit)*. There is a difference between adoration and contemplation. Eucharistic adoration may be personal or communal; in fact, it expresses the full force of what it signifies when an assembly is before the Most Blessed Sacrament, singing, praising, or simply kneeling. The invitatory psalm, with which the Liturgy of the Hours opens every day, aptly expresses the shared character of adoration: "O come, let us worship and bow down, let us kneel before the Lord, our Maker!" (Ps 95:6). Contemplation, instead, is an eminently personal activity; it calls for silence and requires that one be isolated from everything and everyone to concentrate on the object contemplated and to be lost in it. It is this new attitude that the *Adoro Te Devote* invites us to enter into in the two last verses of the first stanza.

To understand the importance accorded to contemplation in the hymn, it is necessary to take into account the ambience and context from which it is born. We are, as I said, this side of the great change in Eucharistic theology occasioned by the reaction to the theories of Berengarius of Tours. The problem on which Christian reflection concentrates almost exclusively is that of the real presence of Christ in the Eucharist, which at times exceeds in the affirmation of a physical and almost material presence.[15] From Belgium came the great wave of Eucharistic fervor, which was soon to spread to the whole of Christianity and led to the institution of the feast of *Corpus Christi* by Pope Urban IV, in 1264.

The sense of respect for the Eucharist increased and, in a parallel manner, so did the sense of the unworthiness of the faithful to approach it, also because of the almost impracticable conditions established to receive Communion (fasting, penance, confession, abstention from conjugal relations). Communion by the people became such a rare event that in 1215 the Fourth Lateran Council had to establish the obligation to go to Communion at least at Easter. But the Eucharist continued to draw souls irresistibly and thus, little by little, the lack of edible contact in Communion was remedied by developing the visible contact of contemplation. (We note that in the East, for the same reasons, the laity were also denied the visible contact because the central rite of the Mass took place behind a curtain, which later became the wall of the iconostasis.)

The elevation of the host and of the chalice at the moment of the consecration (the first written testimony of its institution is in 1196), became, especially for the laity, the most important moment of the Mass, in which their feelings of devotion were poured out and they hoped to receive special graces. It was common for St. Thomas Aquinas himself at the elevation to exclaim the words of the *Te Deum: "Tu*

---

15. The first formula of faith subscribed to by Berengarius held that, in Communion, the body and blood of Christ were present on the altar "sensibly and were in truth touched, and broken by the hands of the priest and chewed by the teeth of the faithful": Denzinger-Schönmetzer, *Enchiridion symbolorum*, 690. St. Thomas Aquinas corrects this affirmation, saying that the body of Christ "is not broken, or shattered or divided by the one who receives it": cf. *S. Th.*, III, q. 77, a. 7.

rex gloriae Christe, tu Patris sempiternus es Filius" ("Thou art the King of glory, O Christ, Thou art the eternal Son of the Father").[16] Bells were rung at that moment to notify those outside the church; some people even used to run from one Mass to another to attend several elevations.[17]

Many Eucharistic hymns were born to accompany this moment; they are hymns for the elevation. To them belongs also our *Adoro Te Devote*, as well as the *Ave Verum*. From beginning to end, its language is that of seeing, contemplating: *te contemplans, non intueor, nunc aspicio, visu sim beatus.*

We no longer have the same conception of the Eucharist; for some time Communion has become an integral part of participation in Mass. The achievements of theology (biblical, liturgical, the ecumenical movement) that came together in the Second Vatican Council and in the liturgical reform have again valued, together with faith in the real presence, other aspects of the Eucharist: the banquet, the sacrifice, the memorial, the communal and ecclesial dimensions.

It might be thought that in this new climate there is no longer a place for the *Adoro Te Devote* and the Eucharistic practices born in that period. Instead, it is precisely now that they are more useful and necessary for us so as not to lose, because of today's achievements, those of yesterday. We cannot reduce the Eucharist only to contemplation of the real presence in the consecrated Host, but it would also be a grave loss to give it up. Pope John Paul II has not ceased to recommend it since his first

---

16. William de Tocco, *Ystoria*, p. 198.
17. Cf. J.-A. Jungmann, *Missarum sollemnia*, III (Paris, 1944), pp. 123–135.

letter to priests, "The Mystery and Worship of the Most Sacred Eucharist," of Holy Thursday of 1980:

> The adoration of Christ in the Sacrament of Love must be expressed in different ways of Eucharistic devotion: personal prayer before the Blessed Sacrament, hours of adoration, and expositions that can be either short, long, or yearly.... The animation and study of the Eucharistic cult are proof of the genuine renewal aimed at by the Council and they are its central point...Jesus awaits us in the Sacrament of Love. Let us find time to meet him in faith-filled adoration and contemplation.[18]

Our Orthodox brothers do not share this aspect of Catholic piety; some of them note that the bread is made to be eaten, not to be looked at. Others, also among Catholics, observe that the practice was developed at a time of grave obscuring of liturgical and sacramental life.

The excellence of Eucharistic contemplation is not based on particular theological explanations but on the impressive testimony of facts, literally "a cloud of testimonies." Innumerable souls attained holiness by practicing it. Among them was Charles de Foucauld, who made adoration of the Eucharistic one of the strong points of his spirituality and of that of his followers. It is a need that touches all categories of persons. This attraction that the Host exercises on souls cannot be explained other than by a special impulse of the Holy Spirit. The Eucharist, within and outside the Mass, has been for the Catholic Church what in the family was, until recently, the domestic hearth during winter: the place around which the family rediscovered its own unity and intimacy, the ideal center of everything.

---

18. John Paul II, *Letter to Priests for Holy Thursday* (1980).

This does not mean that there are not also theological reasons as the basis of Eucharistic contemplation. The first is that which comes from the word of Christ: "Do this in memory of me." In the idea of memorial there is an *objective and sacramental aspect* that consists in repeating the rite completed by Christ, which recalls and renders present his sacrifice. But there is also a *subjective and existential aspect,* which consists in cultivating the memory of Christ, "in having constantly in the memory thoughts that regard Christ and his love."[19] Perhaps both of these elements are present in the expression *"unde et memores"* ("mindful therefore...") of the Roman Canon. This memory of Jesus is not limited to the time that one spends before the tabernacle; it can be cultivated with other means, such as contemplation of icons; but it is true that adoration before the Most Blessed Sacrament is a privileged means to do so.

The two aspects of the memorial—celebration and contemplation of the Eucharist—do not exclude one another, but integrate each other. Contemplation in fact is the means with which we "receive," in a strong sense, the mysteries, with which we interiorize them and open ourselves to their action; it is the equivalent of the mysteries on the existential and subjective plane; it is a way of allowing the grace, received in the sacraments, to mold our inner universe, namely, thoughts, affections, will, memory.

There is a great affinity between the Eucharist and the Incarnation. In the Incarnation, says St. Augustine, "Mary conceived the Word first with her mind then with the body." In fact, he adds, it would have been of no value to her to carry Christ in her womb if she had not carried him

---

19. N. Cabasilas, *Life in Christ,* VI, 4 (PG 150, 653).

with love in her heart.[20] The Christian must also receive Christ in his mind before receiving and after receiving him in his or her body. And to receive Christ in the mind means to contemplate his mysteries, to reflect on his word, to apply it in the situations one is called to live, to listen to the voice of his Spirit, all of which can be done at all times and in all places, but to which his "real presence" confers a unique immediacy and efficacy.

There is another theological reason that justifies Eucharistic adoration. Jesus is present in the Eucharist as God and as man. We proclaim and honor his humanity when we serve him in the poor, in the hungry, and in all those with whom he identified, saying: "You did it to me." We proclaim and honor his divinity when we are in adoration before the sign that renders him present.

It seems clear from all of the above that Eucharistic adoration cannot be detached either from the liturgical and communal celebration of the sacrament or from commitment to the poor and to justice. One draws strength and justification from the other. We witnessed this in Mother Teresa of Calcutta, who in her life gave Eucharistic adoration no less importance than service of the poor and who said that she found in the first the strength to attend to the second. Not all are called to such commitment in either one of these endeavors. However, in a community or a parish one should never exist without the other.

4. Forgetfulness of Everything

Te contemplans: contemplating Thee, says our hymn. What does that pronoun, "Thee," enclose? Surely the

---

20. Cf. Augustine, *On Holy Virginity,* 3 (PL 40, 398).

Christ really present in the Host, but not a static and inert presence; it indicates the whole mystery of Christ, the person and his work; it is listening silently to the Gospel again or to a phrase in the presence of the Author of the Gospel who gives to the word a particular force and immediacy.

But it is not yet the summit of Eucharistic contemplation. This consists essentially in a loving and adoring, penetrating and immobile gaze on Christ who is present. It is an attempt to establish a heart-to-heart contact with Jesus really present in the Host and, through him, to be raised to the Father in the Holy Spirit. In Christianity, contemplation is never one-way; there are two gazes that meet: "He looks at me, I look at him," as the peasant of the parish of Ars famously said to his saintly parish priest. Contemplation is to look at the one who is looking at us.

This stage of contemplation is described by the author of the *Adoro Te Devote* when he affirms: "Everything fails *(deficit)* in contemplating Thee.*" The verb is suggested by Psalm 84:2: "My soul longs, indeed it faints *(deficit)* for the courts of the Lord."

These are words born surely from experience. "Everything fails, everything is silent." What fails? What is silent? Not only does the external world—people and things—but also the internal world of thoughts, images, and worries. "Forgetfulness of everything, except God," wrote Blaise Pascal in his *Memoriale,* describing a similar experience. And Francis of Assisi admonished his brothers: "It is a great misery and a miserable weakness that when you have him present in this way, you are concerned with anything else in the whole world!"[21] *Totum deficit:* everything must be put aside.

Around the same date that our hymn was composed, namely, at the end of the thirteenth century, Roger Bacon, another great lover of the Eucharist, wrote these words that seem like a commentary on the first stanza of the *Adoro Te Devote* and a confirmation of the experience that shines through it:

> If the divine majesty was to manifest itself sensibly, we would not have been able to sustain it and we would have failed all together in reverence, devotion, and wonder. Experience demonstrates it. Those who exercise themselves in the faith and love of this sacrament do not succeed in enduring the devotion that is born from pure faith, without dissolving in tears and without their soul, coming out of itself, liquefying by the sweetness of the devotion, to the point of no longer knowing where they are or why.[22]

Totum deficit!

Eucharistic contemplation is altogether other than indulging in quietism. It was noted how one reflects in him or herself, at times even physically, what he or she contemplates. One is not long exposed to the sun without showing the traces on one's face. Remaining long and with faith, not necessarily with sensible fervor, before the Most Holy Sacrament, we assimilate the thoughts and feelings of Christ, not in a discursive but in an intuitive way, almost *"ex opere operato,"* by the simple fact of being there. In other words, it is what the Apostle Paul says:

---

21. St. Francis, *Letter to the Entire Order* (*Early Documents*, p. 118).

22. Roger Bacon, *Moralis philosophia*, IV (*Opus magnum*, II, ed. J. H. Bridges, Oxford, 1897, p. 402).

"We all, with unveiled faces, beholding the glory of the Lord, are being changed into his likeness from one degree of glory to another; for this comes from the Lord who is the Spirit" (2 Cor 3:18). Every being is shaped by what it contemplates: this insight of the ancient philosopher Plotinus is true even from a Christian point of view.

Eucharistic contemplation also has an extraordinary power of healing. In the desert God ordered Moses to raise a bronze serpent on a pole. All those who were bitten by poisonous snakes and then looked at the bronze serpent were healed (cf. Nm 21:4–9). Jesus applied the mysterious symbol of the bronze serpent to himself (Jn 3:14). What we should do, then, when afflicted by the venomous bites of pride, sensuality, and all the other illnesses of the soul is not to get lost in vain considerations or seek excuses, but to run before the Most Blessed Sacrament, to look at the Host and let healing pass though the same organ through which evil so often passes: our eyes.

If now, however, from these shafts of light that the hymn's author has made us perceive, we return in thought to our reality and to our poor way of staying before the Eucharist, we risk feeling disheartened and discouraged. We would be altogether mistaken. The only thing the Holy Spirit asks of us is that we give him our time, even if at the beginning it might seem like lost time. I will never forget the lesson that was given to me one day in this regard. I said to God: "Lord, give me fervor and I will give you all the time you desire in prayer." I found the answer in my heart: "Raniero, give me your time and I will give you all the fervor you want in prayer."

Fortunately for us, great Eucharistic poetry did not end with the *Adoro Te Devote*. This is how a Catholic poet, Paul Claudel, reproduces in modern language the same impulses aroused by our hymn:

> Eternity, which you searched for far away, is already
>   accessible to our senses in this life,
> Raise your eyes and look straight ahead, look at the
>   Unleavened Bread in the monstrance, it is there...
> This object in the midst of dry paper flowers, it is
>   supreme Beauty itself,
> These words so worn out that we no longer
>   understand them, it is in them that truth is
>   revealed
> I finally see with my eyes that the supreme possession
>   is possible!
> And not only for the soul, but also for the body!
> The veil of things at one point became transparent for
>   me.
> At last I grasped the essence through the accident![23]

---

23. P. Claudel, *La Messe là-bas,* in *Oeuvre Poétique* (Paris: Gallimard, 1965), p. 509.

II.

The Ear Alone Can Safely Be Believed

The Words of the Consecration

One can speak of the Eucharistic mystery—Cardinal Daneels has written—"in the precise and clear language of exegetes and theologians, which the Church can never do without. But one can also use the language of the heart, of wonder, of love...; the language of the Holy Spirit, who is the very breath of the Church, the language of contemplation."[24] I believe that the beauty of the *Adoro Te Devote* lies in the fact that it brings together in itself, in an unsurpassable way, both of these languages; in it the most lucid theology is coupled with an uninterrupted impulse of the heart.

A certain way of speaking of the Eucharist, full of unction and devotion as well as profound doctrine, set aside by the advent of so-called "scientific" theology, is found in early Eucharistic hymns. It is here that we must seek if we wish to overcome the arid conceptualism that has afflicted

---

24. G. Daneels, in *Eucharistia: Encyclopédie de l'Eucharistie,* ed. M. Brouard (Paris: Éditions du Cerf, 2002), p. 11.

the Sacrament of the Altar following the controversies about it.

Thanksgiving, blessing: these are the meanings contained in the Hebrew word *beraka,* translated into Greek as *eucharistia.* The language that is more suitable, therefore, is that of psalms and praises, of poetry and music, which not only translates concepts, but also feelings and impulses of the heart. In our reflection, therefore, we will have recourse whenever possible to Eucharistic poetry, both ancient and modern.

1. Word and Spirit in the Consecration

> *Visus, tactus, gustus in te fállitur,*
> *sed audítu solo tuto créditur.*
> *Credo quidquid dixit Dei Fílius;*
> *nil hoc verbo veritátis vérius.* [25]

Sight, touch, and taste in Thee are each deceived;
the ear alone most safely is believed:
I believe all the Son of God has spoken,
than Truth's own word there is no truer token.

One of the *Lauds* of Jacopone da Todi, composed around the year 1300, contains a clear allusion to the present stanza of the *Adoro Te Devote.* In it the author construes an argument among the different human senses about the Eucharist: three of them say it is only bread,

---

25. The only observation on the critical text of the second stanza of the *Adoro Te Devote* refers to the last verse. As it is, both in the song and in the recitation, one is obliged by the meter to split in half the word *veritatis (veri - tatis),* therefore the variant seems preferable which changes the order of the words and reads *Nil hoc veritatis verbo verius.* Wilmart, p. 159, reads *"nichil veritatis verbo verius";* I believe that the adjective "this" (*hoc* verbo) must be kept for the reason I shall explain later.

but the ear comes forward and makes them draw back, assuring that "Christ is hidden under this visible form."[26] If this does not suffice to affirm that the hymn is by St. Thomas Aquinas, at least it shows that it is older than was thought up to now, and that it dates back to the last years of the Angelic Doctor's life. If Jacopone da Todi can allude to it as a well-known text, it must have been composed at least some twenty years earlier and enjoyed considerable popularity.

In truth, it is not that the senses of sight, touch, and taste can themselves be deceived about the Eucharistic species, but that we can deceive ourselves in interpreting what they tell us. They are not deceived, because appearances are the proper object of the senses—what is seen, touched, and tasted—and the appearances are really those of bread and wine. "In this sacrament," St. Thomas writes, "there is no deception. In fact, the accidents that are perceived by the senses really exist, while the intellect, whose object is the essence of things, is kept from falling into deception by faith."[27] Only later, in the wake of Cartesian philosophy, were there theologians who suggested a different explanation, stating that the Eucharistic species have no objective consistency, but are simply modifications produced by God or by Christ's body itself on our senses. In this case our senses would certainly deceive themselves, but not in St.Thomas' theology.

---

26. Jacopone da Todi, *The Lauds*, 46, trans. S. and E. Hughes (New York: Paulist Press, 1982), p. 158: "Four of the senses concur: this is bread as we know it. / The sense of hearing alone dissents— / Christ is hidden under this visible form." Cf. F. J. E. Raby, *The Date and Authorship of the Poem* Adoro Te Devote, in "Speculum," 20, 1945, pp. 236–238. The text confirms, in the first stanza, the lection *"quae sub his formis"* instead of *"quae sub his figuris."*

27. Aquinas, *S. Th.*, III, q. 75, a. 5, ad. 2.

The phrase "the ear alone most safely is believed," *"auditu solo tuto creditor,"* refers to the affirmation of Romans 10:17, which in the Vulgate reads: *"Fides ex auditu"* ("faith comes from hearing"). Here, however, it is not about listening to God's word in general, but about hearing a precise word pronounced by him who is Truth itself.[28] It is clear which word it refers to: the word of the institution that the priest repeats in the Mass: "This is my body" *(Hoc est corpus meum);* "This is the cup of my blood" *(Hic est calix sanguinis mei).* The author of the *Pange Lingua* alludes to this same "word" when he says that "Word-made-Flesh, the bread of nature / *by his word* to Flesh he turns."[29]

All of this is confirmed by a passage of St. Thomas' *Summa* that our hymn seems to have simply changed into poetry:

> That the real body and blood of Christ is present in this sacrament is something that cannot be perceived either with the senses or with the intellect, but only with faith, which is supported by the authority of God. Because of this, when commenting on the passage in St. Luke 22:19: *"This is my body which is given up for you,"* St. Cyril says: "Do not cast doubt on the truth of this, but rather accept with faith the words of the Savior: because he, being the Truth, does not lie."[30]

The Church has based herself on this word of Christ in explaining the Eucharist; it is the rock of our faith in

---

28. This is why it is important to keep the demonstrative adjective *"this* word," *hoc verbo,* in the last verse (see n. 25).

29. *Verbum caro panem verum / verbo carne efficit.*

30. Aquinas, *S. Th.,* III, q. 75, a. 1.

the real presence. In the Latin world, St. Ambrose had a decisive influence in explaining the nature of this word of Christ:

> When one arrives at the moment of realizing the venerable sacrament, the priest no longer uses his words, but those of Christ. Therefore, it is the word that effects *(conficit)* the sacrament.... The Lord commanded and the heavens were made, he commanded and everything began to exist. See how effective *(operatorius)* Christ's speaking is. Before the consecration, the body of Christ was not there, but after the consecration, I tell you that the body of Christ is now there. He said and it was done, he commanded and it was created (cf. Ps 33:9).[31]

St. Ambrose says that the word, "This is my Body," is an "operative," effective word. The difference between a *speculative* or theoretical proposition (for example, "man is a rational animal"), and an *operative* or practical proposition (for example: *fiat lux,* let there be light) is that the first contemplates the thing as already existing, while the second makes it exist, calls it into being.

If there is something to add to St. Ambrose's explanation and to the words of our hymn, it is that the "operative force" exercised by the word of Christ is owed to the Holy Spirit. It was the Holy Spirit who gave force to the words pronounced in life by Christ, as he himself declared on one occasion to his enemies (cf. Mt 12:28). It is in the Holy Spirit, says the Letter to the Hebrews, that he "offered himself to God" in his passion (cf. Heb 9:14) and it is in that same Spirit that he renews his offering sacramentally at every Mass.

---

31. St. Ambrose, *On the Sacraments,* IV, 14–15.

In the whole Bible one notes a wonderful synergy between the word of God, the *dabar,* and the breath, the *ruah,* that vivifies it and carries it: "By the *word* of the Lord the heavens were made, by the *breath* of his mouth all their host" (Ps 33:6); "His *word* will be a rod that will smite the violent one, with the *breath* of his lips he shall slay the wicked" (Is 11:4). How can one think that this mutual interpenetration is interrupted precisely in the culminating moment of the history of salvation?

Initially, this was a common conviction, both of the Latin as well as the Greek Fathers. The affirmation of St. Cyril of Jerusalem—"it is the Holy Spirit who makes the bread the body of Christ and the wine his blood"[32]—is echoed in the West by St. Augustine: "The visible gifts brought by the hands of man are sanctified to become this great sacrament by the operation of the Spirit of God."[33] It was the deterioration of relations between the two Churches that led each to stiffen its own position and to make this also a point of contention. In order to oppose those who held that "only by virtue of the Holy Spirit the bread becomes the body of Christ," the Latins, basing themselves on the authority of St. Ambrose, ended by insisting exclusively on the words of the consecration.[34]

From the moment that the undue attempt was given up to determine "the precise instant" in which the conversion of the species takes place and, more correctly, consideration was given to the whole of the rite and the intention of the Church in carrying it out, there was a rap-

---

32. St. Cyril of Jerusalem, *Mystagogical Catecheses,* V, 7 (PG 33, 1113ff.).

33. Augustine, *On the Trinity,* III, 4, 10 (PL 42, 874).

34. Cf. Aquinas, *S. Th.,* III, q. 78, a. 4.

prochement between the Orthodox and the Catholic Church. On this point, each one also recognizes the validity of the other's Eucharist. Words of the institution and invocations of the Spirit, together, operate the miracle.

If the Holy Spirit is absent in the *Adoro Te Devote* at the level of explicit reflection, it should be noted, however, that the whole hymn is permeated with his "anointing." The fervor and warm devotion that characterize it can only be explained as the fruit of the Spirit. From this point of view, in fact, the *Adoro Te Devote* can be useful to us so that we do not make the Holy Spirit only a corrective and addition to our Eucharistic theology. It is not enough to shed light on the objective meaning of the *epiclesis* and the role of the Holy Spirit in realizing the sacrament if it is absent or not operative in the heart of the one who celebrates or receives it.

2. Transubstantiation and Transignification

Without using the term, this stanza of the hymn encloses the doctrine of transubstantiation, that is, as defined by the Council of Trent, the "admirable and singular conversion of the whole substance of the bread and the whole substance of the wine into the body and blood of our Lord Jesus Christ."[35]

Is it possible today to render this philosophical term comprehensible, outside of the small circle of specialists? I tried it once in a television broadcast on the Gospel, giving an example that I hope will not be irreverent. When one sees a woman coming out of a hairdresser's with a totally new hairdo, one spontaneously exclaims: "What a

---

35. Denzinger-Schönmetzer, no. 1652.

transformation!" No one dreams of exclaiming "What transubstantiation!" Rightly so. Changed in fact are the form and external aspect, but not the profound being and personality. If the woman was intelligent before, she is still so now; if she was not so before, she is not so now. The appearances have changed, not the substance.

The exact opposite happens in the Eucharist: the substance changes, but not the appearances. The bread is transubstantiated, but not (at least in this sense) transformed; the appearances, in fact (form, taste, color, weight) remain as before, while the profound reality is changed. It has become the body of Christ. Jesus' promise has been realized: "The bread that I shall give is my flesh for the life of the world" (Jn 6:51).

In recent times, theology has pursued this same attempt to translate the concept of transubstantiation into a modern language, with very different instrumentation and earnestness, appealing to the existential categories of transignification and transfinalization. With these words is designated "the divine (not human) act in which the substance (that is, the meaning and the power) of a religious sign is transformed into the personal revelation of God."[36]

The attempt stems from the conviction that the Eucharist is not just a thing, but also an action, a sign. It is "the action of Christ associating the Church with himself in his timeless worship of the Father," and that "a myopic concentration on the substance of the bread and the substance of the body of Christ ends up with a cosmological miracle devoid of any significant religious setting."[37]

---

36. J. M. Powers, *Eucharistic Theology* (New York: Herder and Herder, 1967), p. 171.

37. Ibid., pp. 174–175.

As always, the attempt did not succeed at first. In some authors' writings (not in all) these new perspectives, more than explaining transubstantiation, ended by replacing it. In this connection, in the encyclical *Mysterium Fidei* Paul VI disapproves of the terms "transignification" and "transfinalization"; more precisely, he disapproved, as he wrote, "of those who limit themselves to use only these terms, without also making use of the word 'transubstantiation.'"[38]

In fact, the Pope himself makes it clear, in the very same encyclical, how these new concepts may be useful if they seek to bring to light new and current aspects and implications of the concept of transubstantiation without attempting to replace it. He wrote:

> As a result of transubstantiation, the species of bread and wine undoubtedly take on a new signification and a new finality, for they are no longer ordinary bread and wine but instead a sign of something sacred and a sign of spiritual food; but they take on this new signification, this new finality, precisely because they contain a new "reality" which we can rightly call ontological.[39]

He himself expressed this with greater clarity in a homily on the Solemnity of *Corpus Christi* when he was archbishop of Milan:

> Christ wished to choose this sacred symbol of human life, which bread is, to make an even more sacred symbol of himself. He has transubstantiated it, but has not taken away its expressive power; rather, *he has elevated this expressive power to a new meaning*, a higher meaning, a mystical, religious, divine meaning. He has

---

38. See *Mysterium Fidei*, no. 11.
39. Ibid., no. 46.

made of it a ladder for an ascent that transcends the natural level. As a sound becomes a voice, and as the voice becomes word, thought, truth; so that sign of the bread has passed from its humble and pious being to signify a mystery; it has become a sacrament; it has acquired the power to demonstrate the body of Christ present.[40]

Catholic theology has sought to reflect on again and study more deeply the concept of transignification and transfinalization in light of Paul VI's reservations. If the changing of meaning and end of the bread and wine also entails a change of substance, as called for by fidelity to the term transubstantiation, it depends on the concept one has of substance. This has changed profoundly in modern physics and philosophy, as Pope Paul VI himself took into account when he specified that in Eucharistic usage the philosophical terms "are not tied to a certain specific form of human culture, or to a certain level of scientific progress, or to one or another theological school. Instead, they set forth what the human mind grasps of reality through necessary and universal experience."[41] This seems to allow one to take into consideration what common sense means today by "the substance" of a thing. Tillard writes:

> From this point of view, substance is that which the intelligence intuits and recognizes under the ensemble of appearances, and of that which strikes the senses. Now before the anaphora, to the question "what is that thing

---

40. G. B. Montini, *Pane celeste e vita sociale* (Bread from Heaven and Social Life), in *"Rivista Diocesana Milanese,"* 1959, p. 428ff, reproduced in *Il Gesù di Paolo VI,* ed. V. Levi (Milan: Mondadori, 1985), p. 189.

41. *Mysterium Fidei,* no. 24.

on the table?" the believer responds: "It is bread." After the anaphora the believer responds: "It is the body
of Christ, true bread of life" ... The bread has not only
changed its destination and end. For the believer's in-
telligence, even if nothing has changed physically, it is
no longer what it was at first: it has become the body
of Christ. His profound being—Scholasticism and Trent
say the substance—is changed.... Bread and wine remain food, but it is no longer substantially the same
nutriment. Christ is there to communicate himself, under a sacramental way of being.[42]

Perhaps, despite these efforts, we have not yet arrived
at an ideal solution that responds to all the exigencies, but
one cannot give up the effort to "inculturate" faith in the
Eucharist in today's world, as the Fathers of the Church and
St. Thomas Aquinas did, each in their own time and culture. If one considers substance as commonly used today,
it becomes difficult to accept that bread, which eaten in
quantity satiates, and wine, which drunk in quantity ine-
briates, do not have substance of their own. On the contrary, it is currently said that such bread is "substantial"!

It is hoped that the Synod of Bishops on "The Eucharist: Source and Summit of the Life and Mission of the
Church," will make some contribution in this direction. In
fact, it is not possible to keep the understanding of the Eucharist alive and new in the Church of today if we remain
at the stage of theological reflection attained many centuries ago, as if exegesis, biblical theology, the ecumenical
movement, and dogmatic theology itself had not contributed anything new in this field in the meantime. In ad-

---

42. J. M. R. Tillard, in *Eucharistia: Encyclopédie de l'Eucharistie*, ed.
M. Brouard (Paris: Éditions du Cerf, 2002), p. 407.

dressing the new attempts to explain the Eucharistic mystery we must apply the principle of discernment indicated by the Apostle: "test everything; hold fast what is good" (1 Thes 5:21).

From the rediscovery of the importance of signs in the Eucharist, we can draw an immediate consequence. If the signs of bread and wine are something more than "accidents" they must be as recognizable and transparent as possible. It is important, for example, that the host really makes one think of bread and not of paper, as is the case with some hosts still widely in use. ("Why didn't the priest give me a piece of paper too?" said a child whose mother had just received Communion!)

If the Eucharist is a banquet, it is necessary—as is true in every banquet—that all the guests be offered not only something to eat, but also something to drink, that is, the possibility of also receiving the blood of Christ. Moreover, to respect the sign of the banquet, one should avoid consecrating great quantities of hosts in a Mass to distribute them to the faithful later in the week, after the priest has consumed the one just consecrated. It would be as if at a banquet the master of the house served himself the food just cooked and then sent for the leftovers of the day before to offer them to the other guests.

3. Body Given, Blood Shed

I said earlier that the words of the institution of the Supper are the rock on which rests the faith of the Catholic Church in the real presence of Christ in the Eucharist. These words are, however, much more than this, and we would lose the essence of the mystery if we limited it to this. In pronouncing those words, Jesus did not intend to give proof of his real presence, as though anticipating future discussions among his disciples in this respect. When saying: "This is my body given up for you.... This is my blood shed for you," he offered himself to the Father in sacrifice for humanity; he accepted the fate of the Servant of Yahweh that the Father had announced to him at the moment of his baptism in the Jordan, yet this time not as a distant and uncertain prospect, but as a concrete and imminent reality.

This is the interior act that accompanies the words of the institution, which the rite must serve to maintain perpetually alive and present among his disciples until his return. In this connection, it is common today to say that the Eucharist is not primarily the real presence of a *thing* (the body and blood of Christ), but of an *action* (the offering that Christ makes of his own body and his own blood).

The words of Christ: "This is the cup of my blood which is shed for you," are the proof (which no criticism has been able to undermine until now) that he accepted and gave a very precise meaning to his death, independently of the intentions of those who decided on it and of the external circumstances in which it occurred. He did not simply suffer it, but he accepted it. In this sense the Eucharist is also a "testament," the "new and eternal testament," that contains the "last will" of Christ.

The incommensurable greatness of the Eucharist lies in the fact that it allows all those who participate in it with faith to be "present" at the absolute summit of the spiritual history of the world, in which truly "everything has been accomplished." This explains why those to whom it has been given to live this moment of the Mass intensely are sometimes overwhelmed by its greatness. Whoever attended a Mass celebrated by Padre Pio of Pietrelcina no doubt remembers what happened in the assembly when he came to the consecration and seemed unable to continue.

Saints and children are needed to break the habit. A father told me the following story. His four- or five-year-old son was at Mass with him and, like all children, moved around and was restless. At the moment of the consecration, he made a severe sign to the boy, asking him to stay still and to be good. The child obeyed, but on hearing the priest's words he burst out crying and he continued to sob until the end. After leaving the church, the father asked the child why he cried. Astonished, his son answered: "But didn't you hear the priest say that someone was dying?" The child had heard: "This is my blood poured out for you" and had given the words their obvious meaning.

From all this one can see even the existential meaning that the Eucharist can have for the believer. Christ's example is an invitation not to wait for age, circumstances, or men's violence to dispose of our life, and to die "without having made a will," without having freely and consciously stated the meaning we gave to our life, for whom we have lived, and for whom we wish to die.

4. Mystery of Faith

We will now look at the response the author of the hymn invites us to cry out with him to the truth enunciated. It is condensed in one word: *Credo!* I believe! *Credo quidquid dixit Dei Filius,* I believe all the Son of God has said. At the end of the consecration of the chalice (in the old Roman Missal, specifically in the middle of it) resounds the exclamation: *Mysterium fidei!* Mystery of faith!

To believe, in this case, means to make oneself contemporary with the event, and to make oneself contemporary with the event means to listen to the words, "Take, eat; take, drink," and to realize, by a sudden illumination, that it is the Risen One who speaks and that such words are addressed personally to you and those next to you, here and now.

"Do not open wide the mouth, but the heart," St. Augustine said. "We are not nourished by what we see, but by what we believe."[43] Faith is necessary if one is to have a true "contact" with the body of Christ. This was also true during Jesus' life. One day a woman approached him, certain that if she only touched the fringe of his garment she would be healed of her hemorrhage. Jesus turned to see who had touched him; the disciples quite rightly pointed out to him: "The multitudes surround you and press upon you and you say: who was it that touched me?" But Jesus insisted: "Someone touched me; for I perceive that power has gone forth from me" (Lk 8:45ff.). It is one thing to touch Christ only with the body; it is quite another thing to touch him also with the soul. "He touches Christ who believes in Christ."[44]

In the Eucharist also, it is only by faith that a spiritual, and not just physical, contact is realized with Jesus and that divine energies are received, which emanate from his body. From contact with the Savior's body the woman hoped to be healed from the flow of blood,

43. Augustine, *Sermo* 112, 5 (PL 38, 645).

44. Augustine, *Sermo* 243, 2 (PL 38, 1144): *"Tangit Christum, qui credit in Christum."*

and we can hope to be healed from the relentless flow of vain thoughts, distractions, and all other spiritual hemorrhages.

But what, exactly, is the meaning of the exclamation "mystery of faith" in the Mass? With this expression, they probably wished to affirm, at the beginning, that "the Eucharist contains and unveils all the economy of the redemption."[45] It summarizes and updates the whole Christian mystery. "Every time that the memorial of this sacrifice is celebrated," says a prayer of the *Gelasian Sacramentary* still in use today, "the work of our redemption is accomplished."[46] *"Mysterium fidei!"* When the priest recites or chants these words, all present acclaim: "We proclaim your death, O Lord, and we proclaim your resurrection, until you come in glory." The Eucharist is truly "the whole in the fragment."

It is necessary to continually reawaken "the Eucharistic amazement."[47] "You alone, my God, be responsible for this enormity, which is too great for me." So Paul Claudel, a poet, expressed his wonder before the Eucharist.[48] The Eucharist is literally an "enormity," something that goes beyond all that man considers "normal" in the way God acts toward man.

The most serious risk we run is to grow accustomed to the Eucharist, to take it for granted and, therefore, to trivialize it. Every so often, even among us, the cry of John the Baptist should resound: "Among you stands one

---

45. Cf. M. Righetti, *Storia liturgica*, III (Milan, 1966), p. 396 (the explanation is by B. Botte).

46. See prayers for the Second Sunday of Ordinary Time.

47. John Paul II, *Ecclesia de Eucharistia* (2003), no. 6.

48. P. Claudel, *Hymne du Saint Sacrement*, in *Oeuvre poétique complète* (Paris, 1967), p. 402.

whom you do not know!" (Jn 1:26). We are rightly horrified at the news of violated tabernacles, ciboria stolen for abominable ends. Perhaps Jesus repeats what he said of his executioners: "They know not what they do." But perhaps what most saddens him is the coldness of his own. To them—that is, to us—he repeats the words of the psalm: "It is not an enemy who taunts me—then I could bear it...but it is you, my equal, my companion, my familiar friend" (Ps 54 [55]:13–14). In the revelations to St. Margaret Mary Alacoque, Jesus did not lament so much the sins of the atheists of the time as he did the indifference and coldness of souls consecrated to him.

The Lord made use of a non-believing woman to make me understand what should be the experience of one who takes the Eucharist seriously. Although she was an atheist, I gave this woman a book to read on this subject, seeing her interest in this religious problem. After one week, she returned the book to me saying: "You have not put a book in my hands but a bomb... Do you realize the enormity of the thing? Absorbing what is written here, it would be enough to open one's eyes to discover that there is altogether another world around us; that the blood of a man who died 2,000 years ago saves all of us. Do you know that, when I read it, my legs were trembling and every now and then I had to stop reading and get up. If it is true, it changes everything."

In listening to her, along with the joy of seeing that the seed had not been sown in vain, I felt a great sense of humiliation and shame. I had received Communion a few minutes before, but my legs were not trembling. The atheist was not all wrong who said one day to a believing friend: "If I could believe that the Son of God is really in that host, as you say, I think I would fall down on my knees and never get up."

The stanza of the *Adoro Te Devote*, which we have commented on, closely recalls two stanzas of the *Pange Lingua*, one of which is the famous *Tantum Ergo*, sung in every Eucharistic Benediction. It also attributes to the word of Christ the changing of the bread and wine into his body and blood. We are exhorted to place our trust in faith, not in the senses. We could even sing by ourselves the two stanzas, seeking to express through it our faith and our "Eucharistic amazement":

> Word-made-Flesh, the bread of nature
> by his word to Flesh he turns;
> wine into his Blood he changes;
> what though sense no change discerns?
> Only be the heart in earnest,
> faith her lesson quickly learns.

> Down in adoration falling,
> Lo! the sacred Host we hail;
> Lo! o'er ancient forms departing,
> newer rites of grace prevail;
> faith for all defects supplying,
> where the feeble senses fail.

III.

Here Lies Hid
the Manhood Too

Divinity and Humanity of Christ in the Eucharist

Nothing disconcerts the human mind more regarding God's action, Tertullian noted, than the disproportion between the simplicity of the means used and the greatness of the effects obtained. It is the exact opposite of what occurs in human works.[49] This characteristic of divine action shines in a particular way in the Eucharist: a few pieces of bread and some drops of wine, accompanied by some words, and the whole mystery of salvation is rendered present, the Church congregated, the soul filled with grace. The greatest merit of the *Adoro Te Devote* is precisely that of reflecting this characteristic. With a few simple words it says the most sublime things about the Eucharist.

---

49. Cf. Tertullian, *On Baptism,* 2 (CCL 1, p. 277).

1. Contemporaries of the Good Thief

We now turn to the third stanza of the hymn, which we will reflect on in this meditation:

> *In cruce latébat sola déitas*
> *at hic latet simul et humánitas;*
> *Ambo tamen credens atque cónfitens*
> *peto quod petívit latro poénitens.*

> God only on the cross lay hid from view;
> but here lies hid at once the Manhood too;
> and I, in both professing my belief,
> make the same prayer as the repentant thief.

In the third stanza of the *Adoro Te Devote* the author goes spiritually to Calvary. In a subsequent stanza, which begins with the words, *"O memoriale mortis Domini,"* he contemplates the intrinsic and objective relationship between the Eucharist and the cross, the relationship, that is, which exists between the event and the sacrament. Here, rather, is expressed the subjective relationship between that which occurred in those who were present at the Lord's death and that which must occur also in one who is present at the Eucharist; the relationship between the one who lived the event and the one who celebrates the sacrament.

It is an invitation to become "contemporaries" of the event commemorated in the intense and existential sense of the term. To consider Christ's death not in the light of hindsight, but to identify with those who lived, in all its rawness, the "scandal" of the cross, leaving out of consideration, at least for the moment, the aura of glory that the resurrection has conferred on it.

Among all those present at Calvary, the author chooses one person in particular, the good thief, with whom to identify. A profound and genuine sentiment of humility and contrition pervades the whole stanza. In the allusive style of the hymn, the author invokes the whole episode of the good thief and all the words he pronounces on the cross, not only the final prayer: "Jesus, remember me when you come into your Kingdom."

He first of all rebukes his companion who insults Jesus: "Do you not fear God, since you are under the same sentence of condemnation? And we indeed justly; for we are receiving the due reward of our deeds; but this man has done nothing wrong" (Lk 23:40ff.). The good thief makes a complete confession of sin. His repentance is of the purest biblical quality. True repentance consists in accusing oneself and exonerating God, attributing to oneself the responsibility of evil and proclaiming that "God is innocent." The constant formula of repentance in the Bible is: "You are just in everything that you have done, straight are your ways and just your judgments, we have sinned" (cf. Dn 3:28ff.; cf. Dt 32:4ff.).

"He has done nothing wrong": In these words, the good thief (or, in any case, the Holy Spirit who inspired these words) shows himself to be an excellent theologian. Only God, in fact, suffers as innocent; every other being who suffers must say: "I suffer justly," because, even if he is not responsible for the action that is imputed to him, he is never altogether without fault.[50] Only the pain of innocent children is like that of God and that is why it is so mysterious and so precious.

---

50. Cf. S. Kierkegaard, *Edifying discourses in various spirit*, 3: *The Gospel of suffering*, IV.

The good thief's confession of sin was the penitential rite of the first Mass, celebrated not sacramentally, but in reality on the cross. The liturgy invites us to imitate it; we also make our confession of sin at the beginning of every Eucharistic celebration. One of the invocations in the Missal for the penitential act says: "Lord, who promised paradise to the repentant thief, have mercy on us." In some liturgies, this spirit of contrition accompanies the whole celebration. Whoever has been to a Russian liturgy will recall the exclamation *"Gòspodi pomilui, Gòspodi pomilui"* ("Lord, have mercy, Lord, have mercy") that is repeated incessantly in the course of the rite. The same thing occurred in the past in the Ambrosian liturgy, with the repetition of the *Kyrie eleison* at several moments of the Mass.

However, even here a correct balance must be maintained and, in this respect, the Roman liturgy is a model. The feeling of one's sinfulness and unworthiness does not extend throughout the celebration; it is stated at the beginning and recalled at the moment of Communion with the words, *"Domine non sum dignus"* ("Lord, I am not worthy..."). We know the inconvenience created in the past by a too exclusive sense of one's unworthiness inculcated in the faithful. This ended by keeping people away from Communion. We must never forget what Jesus said to those who reproached him for being seated at table with sinners: "Those who are well have no need of a physician, but those who are sick" (Mt 9:12).

When, after walking long on muddy streets, we arrive at the door of the Church, observes Charles Péguy, it is right to clean our feet and shake off the mud from our shoes. But, once inside, we should not spend the whole time looking at our feet to see if they are clean or dirty.

Heart, eyes, voice, everything must now tend toward "the altar on which the body of Jesus and the memory and expectation of him shine eternally." To take into the church the memory and thought of the mud would be to take mud into the church.[51]

2. Body, Blood, Soul, and Divinity

There is a profound analogy between the good thief and the one who approaches the Eucharist with faith. The good thief on the cross saw a man condemned to death, and he believed that he was God, acknowledging his power to remember him in his Kingdom. From a certain point of view, the Christian is called to make an even more difficult act of faith. "On the cross only the divinity was hidden; here, however, even the humanity is concealed."

The one praying does not hesitate an instant; he rises to the height of the good thief's faith and proclaims that he believes in both the divinity and humanity of Christ: *"Ambo tamen credens atque cónfitens."* Two verbs: *credo, confiteor,* I believe and I profess. It is not a repetition. St. Paul has illustrated the difference between believing and confessing: "For man believes with his heart and so is justified, and he confesses with his lips and so is saved" (Rom 10:10).

It is not enough to believe in the depth of one's heart; it is also necessary to profess one's faith publicly. At the time our hymn was written, the Church had just instituted the feast of *Corpus Christi* precisely with this objective. After all, the memory of the institution of the Eucharist on Holy Thursday already existed. If the Church instituted

---

51. C. Péguy, *Le mystère des Saints Innocents, Oeuvres poétiques complètes* (Paris: Gallimard, 1975), p. 689ff.

this new feast, it was not so much to commemorate the event as to publicly proclaim faith in the real presence of Christ in the Eucharist. And, as a matter of fact, with the extraordinary solemnity that it assumed and the manifestations that characterized it in Christian piety (processions, floral decorations, etc.), the feast precisely fulfilled this objective.

The central theological truth in this stanza (every stanza, we noted, has one) is that in the Eucharist Christ is really present with his divinity and humanity, "in body, blood, soul, and divinity," according to the traditional formula. It is worthwhile to reflect on this formula and its assumptions, because, in this regard, modern biblical theology has contributed some novelties that must be taken into account.

Scholastic theology affirmed that, by the words, "This is my body," only the body of Christ—namely his flesh, composed of bones, nerves, etc.—is made present on the altar "by the power of the sacrament" (vi sacramenti), while his blood and soul are present only by dint of the principle of "natural concomitance," according to which, where there is a living body, there is necessarily also blood and soul. Similarly, by the words, "This is my blood," by the power of the sacrament only his blood is made present, while the body and soul are there by natural concomitance.[52]

All these problems are due to the fact that "body" is understood as interpreted in Greek anthropology, namely, as that part of man that, united to the soul and the in-

---

52. Cf. Aquinas, S. Th., III, q. 76, a. 1. The principle of natural concomitance was taken up by the Council of Trent (Denzinger-Schünmetzer, 1640), which, however, on this point simply quoted St. Thomas, without giving this explanation dogmatic value.

telligence, forms the complete man. The progress of biblical sciences, however, has made us aware that in biblical language, which is the language of Jesus and Paul, "body" does not indicate, as for us today, a third of the person, but the whole person inasmuch as he or she lives in a bodily dimension. In Eucharistic contexts "body" has the same meaning that the word "flesh" has in John. We know what John means when he says that the Word was made "flesh"—not that he was made "flesh, bones, nerves," but that he was made man. The liberating conclusion is that the soul of Christ is not present in the Eucharist somewhat indirectly, only by natural concomitance with the body, but directly, by the power of the sacrament, being included in what Jesus understood when speaking of his body.

If one understands "body" in the Greek philosophical sense, it becomes difficult to refute the objection: What need was there to consecrate the blood separately from the moment that it is but a part of the body, the same as the bones, nerves, and other organs? The answer once given to this objection was the following: "Because, in the passion of Christ, of which the sacrament is a memorial, no other component was separated from his body except the blood."[53] But can this explanation still satisfy?

A much simpler explanation is that in the Bible the blood is the seat of life and the effusion of blood is, therefore, the eloquent sign of death. The consecration of the blood is explained taking into account that the sacraments are sacred signs and Jesus chose such a sign to leave us a living "memorial of his passion." For our consolation, body, blood, and soul, all therefore, are present in the

---

53. Aquinas, *S. Th.*, III, q. 76, a. 2, ad. 2.

Eucharist by the power of the very words of Christ, not by some philosophical principle derived from Aristotle.

3. Born to Be Able to Die

In our hymn all of these problems are absent and all is soberly reduced to the presence of the humanity and divinity of Christ in the Eucharist. The presence of the divinity, whether in the body or the blood of Christ, is assured by the indissoluble union (hypostatic, in theological language) realized between the Word and humanity in the Incarnation. Therefore, the Eucharist cannot be explained other than in the light of the Incarnation; it is, so to speak, its sacramental prolongation.

"The Eucharist," says John Paul II in his encyclical *Ecclesia de Eucharistia,* "while commemorating the passion and resurrection, is also in continuity with the Incarnation. At the annunciation, Mary conceived the Son of God in the physical reality of his body and blood, thus anticipating within herself what to some degree happens sacramentally in every believer who receives, under the signs of bread and wine, the Lord's body and blood."[54]

The Eucharist brings Christmas and Easter together, actualizing the birth and death of Christ. A certain romantic tendency has succeeded in making Christmas a wholly human feast of maternity and childhood, of gifts and of good sentiments. In Moscow's Tetriakov Gallery, the icon of the "Virgin of Tenderness" that depicts her pressing the baby Jesus to herself, bore the caption "Maternity" during the Communist regime. However, experts know what is signified in the Mother's worried look,

---

54. *Ecclesia de Eucharistia,* no. 55.

tinged with sadness, as if wishing to protect her child from impending danger. The iconographer's intention is to announce the passion of the Son, which Simeon made her perceive in the presentation in the Temple.

Christian art has expressed this connection between the birth and death of Christ in a thousand ways. In some pictures by famous artists, the child Jesus sleeps on his Mother's knees stretched out on a cloth, in the exact position in which he is usually represented in the deposition from the cross; the bound lamb that is often seen in representations of the Nativity alludes to the immolated Lamb. In a fifteenth-century painting, one of the Wise Men gives the child Jesus the gift of a chalice with coins in it—a sign of the price of the ransom he came to pay for sins. (The child is in the act of taking one of the coins and handing it to the one who offers it to him, a sign that he will die for him also!)[55]

In this way, the artists express a profound theological truth. "The Word became flesh," writes St. Augustine, "to be able to die for us."[56] He is born to be able to die. In the Gospels themselves the accounts of the childhood are a preamble to the accounts of the passion.

4. One Believes with the Heart

We now move from the theological affirmation to the application in prayer, a movement present in every stanza of the *Adoro Te Devote*. The existential implication in this

---

55. The paintings on this topic constituted a section of the exhibition entitled "Seeing Salvation," held in London in the year 2000 and reproduced in part in the exhibition's catalogue: cf. *The Images of Christ* (London, 2000), pp. 62–73.

56. Augustine, *Sermo* 23A, 3 (CCL 41, 322); Gregory of Nyssa affirms the same, *Oratio catechetica*, 32 (PG 45, 80).

case is the invitation to a renewed act of faith in the full humanity and divinity of Christ. The first stanza also contains a profession of faith: *"Credo quidquid dixit Dei Filius,"* ("I believe everything that the Son of God has spoken"). But there it was only a question of faith in the real presence of Christ in the sacrament. Here the problem is knowing who it is who makes himself present on the altar; the object of faith here is the person of Christ, not the sacramental action.

Credens atque confitens: I believe and profess. We said that it was not enough to believe; we must also profess. We must immediately add: it is not enough to profess, we must also believe! The most frequent sin of the laity is to believe without professing, hiding their faith out of human respect (the familiar non-practicing believers); the most frequent sin in us, men of the Church, might be that of professing without believing. In fact, it is possible that little by little faith becomes a "creed" that is repeated with the lips, as a declaration of belonging, a flag, without ever asking oneself if one really believes what one says. *Corde creditur,* Paul has reminded us, a phrase that St. Augustine translates as: "Faith rises from the roots of the heart."[57]

It is necessary, however, to distinguish lack of faith from the darkness of faith and temptations against it. We have an example of this in the life of the Precursor of Christ. One day John the Baptist sent two of his disciples to ask Jesus: "Are you he who is to come, or shall we look for another?" (Mt 11:3). We should not overlook the drama that is hidden behind this episode in the Precursor's life. He is in prison, cut off from everything; he knows

---

57. Augustine, *On the Gospel of John,* 26, 2 (PL 35, 1077).

that his life is hanging by a thread; but the external darkness is nothing compared to the darkness that arises in his
heart. He no longer knows if all that he has lived for is
true or false. He had pointed out the Rabbi of Nazareth as
the Messiah, as the Lamb of God, and pressed the people
and also his disciples to follow him, and now he suffers
the piercing doubt that all this might have been an error,
that Jesus is not the one awaited. How different is this
John the Baptist from the one at the beginning of the
Gospel, thundering on the banks of the Jordan!

But how is it that Jesus, who seems so severe in face of
the people's lack of faith and who reproaches his disciples
for being "men of little faith," shows himself, in this circumstance, so understanding of his Precursor's uncertainty?
He does not refuse to provide the "signs" requested, as he
does in other cases: "Go and tell John what you hear and
see...." The envoys having left, Jesus expresses of the Baptist the greatest praise that ever came from his lips: "Among
those born of women there has risen no one greater than
John the Baptist," adding only in that circumstance:
"Blessed is he who takes no offense at me" (Mt 11:6). He
knew how easy it was to "take offense" at him, in his apparent impotence, in the apparent denial of the facts.

The Baptist's test is one that is renewed in every age,
especially in the life of one who, like him, must repeat
every day, holding the host in his hand: "Behold the Lamb
of God!" There have been great souls who lived only by
faith and who, in a phase of their life, often even the last,
fell into the most painful darkness, tormented by the
doubt of having failed in everything and lived in deceit.
There is faith in these cases, stronger than ever, but hidden in a remote corner of the soul, which only God is able

to read. If God so glorified John the Baptist, it means that when he was in darkness he never ceased believing in the Lamb of God whom he once pointed out to the world. The Apostle Paul's testament was also his: "I have finished the race, I have kept the faith" (2 Tm 4:7).

Faith is the wedding ring that unites God and humanity in an alliance. Like gold, faith—says the First Letter of Peter—must be purified in the crucible (cf. 1:7), and the crucible of faith is suffering, above all suffering caused by doubt and by what St. John of the Cross calls the dark night of the spirit. According to the Catholic doctrine of Purgatory, everything can continue to be purified after death—hope, charity, humility—except faith. The latter can only be purified in this life, before passing from faith to vision. This is why the test here below is so often concentrated precisely on faith and at times precisely on faith in the real presence of Christ in the Eucharist.

However, it is not just a question of exceptional souls. The same difficulty that drove the Baptist to send messengers to Jesus still impedes the Jewish people from recognizing Jesus of Nazareth as the awaited Messiah. And not only the Jews—the Second Letter of St. Peter refers to the question that was rife among Christians of his time: "Where is the promise of his coming? For, ever since the fathers fell asleep, all things have continued as they were from the beginning of creation" (3:4). Even today, this is the reason why many people do not believe in an accomplished redemption: "Everything," they say, "continues as before!"

Peter suggests an explanation: God "is not slow about his promise as some count slowness, but is forbearing toward you, not wishing that any should perish, but that all should reach repentance" (2 Pt 3:9). But more than speculative reasons, it is necessary to draw from one's heart the strength that makes faith triumph over doubt and skepticism. It is in the heart that the Holy Spirit makes the believer know that Jesus is alive and real in a way that cannot be expressed by reasoning and that no reasoning can overcome.

At times, one word from Scripture suffices to rekindle this faith and renew the certainty. For me this was settled last Advent by Balaam's oracle: "I see him, but not now; I behold him, but not nigh: a star shall come forth out of Jacob, and a scepter shall rise out of Israel" (Nm 24:17). It was a beam of light, a short circuit between prophecy and realization. We know that star, we know to whom that scepter belongs, not by abstract deduction, but because for 2,000 years the realization of the prophecy has been before our eyes.

The exegetes say that the oracle referred to David, but we know that a text or a work of art can contain more than its creator saw and intended at the moment of creating it. Often, an author must acknowledge this when someone brings to his or her attention an insight he or she had about it. But if this is true for human works, how much more so for a work like the Bible, which is not only of human authors? I continue to believe that we do not deceive ourselves in referring to Jesus this and other oracles of the Old Testament, which we hear in the liturgy during Advent. I believe it because I see what hearing one of their words does for me, illuminating me mysteriously and becoming active within me. Something is renewed every time, akin to what happened to Balaam when pronouncing those words: "a veil is stripped from the eyes" (see Num 24:16).

Scripture, read spiritually throughout the year, leads us into the Eucharistic mystery; the "table of the word" prepares us for the "table of the body." The daily readings of the Mass evoke biblical personalities and events that are imbued with Eucharistic symbolism. Think of Moses before the burning bush, of Isaiah receiving the burning coal on his lips, of Elijah eating the bread baked under the ashes, of Ezekiel swallowing the scroll written on both sides, of Simeon receiving the child in his arms, of the paralytic lowered before Jesus, of Zacchaeus, to whom Jesus says: "Today I must come to your house." Finally, as suggested by the author of the *Adoro Te Devote,* let us recall the good thief on the cross, and Thomas, who touches the wounds.... These are all experiences that remind us of the Eucharist and can be spiritually relived in it.

In this meditation, we have emphasized the relationship between the Eucharist and Christmas. The Eucharist is the true crib in which it is possible to adore the incarnate Word not in images, but in reality. A sign of the continuity between the mystery of the Incarnation and the Eucharistic mystery is that with the same words, in the first stanza of the *Adoro Te Devote,* we use to greet the God hidden under the appearances of bread and wine, we can, at Christmas, use to greet the God hidden under the appearance of a child, without having to change a single syllable.

The same continuity between the birth of Christ, the Eucharist, and the cross is brought to light, with striking conciseness, in another Eucharistic hymn sung at one time before the exposed Blessed Sacrament. With it, we end our meditation in prayer:

Se nascens dedit socium,
convescens in edulium,
se moriens in praetium,
se regnans dat in praemium.

O salutaris hostia,
quae caeli pandis ostium,
bella premunt hostilia:
da robur, fer auxilium.

By birth their fellow-man was he,
their meat, when sitting at the board;
he died, their ransomer to be;
he ever reigns, their great reward.

O saving Victim, opening wide
the gate of heaven to man below,
our foes press on from every side,
Thine aid supply, Thy strength bestow.

IV.

Like Thomas the Apostle

The Eucharist and the Resurrection of Christ

1. With Thomas in the Cenacle

The fourth stanza of the *Adoro Te Devote* closely parallels the preceding one. In the third stanza the author took us to Calvary to make us relive the event of Christ's death. Here he takes us to the Cenacle to have us meet the Risen One. He wishes to show that the Eucharist is in close relationship both with the death and the resurrection of Christ, but he does not do so in theoretical and abstract terms. With felicitous poetic intuition, in both cases he chooses an episode and a concrete character with whom to identify: for the cross, the good thief; and for the resurrection, the apostle Thomas.

> *Plagas sicut Thomas non intúeor;*
> *Deum tamen meum te confíteor.*
> *Fac me tibi semper magis crédere,*
> *in te spem habére, te dilígere.*

Thy wounds, as Thomas saw, I do not see;
yet Thee confess my Lord and God to be:

make me believe Thee ever more and more;
in Thee my hope, in Thee my love to store.

The whole episode of the twofold appearance of the
risen Jesus in the Cenacle, narrated in John, chapter 20, is
recalled with the usual economy of words. In this case also, the secret is to become contemporaries of the event, as
the hymn's author does, to take the apostle's place in this
experience. Jesus takes up the challenge of Thomas, who
said he would not believe without first having seen and
touched the wounds of the Crucified. Christ makes an
unusual exception and concession to the apostle, inviting
him to look and touch, something he did not do with
Magdalene, to whom he said: "Do not touch me!" The
Master's condescension makes the apostle rise at once to
a level of faith that had never been attained until that moment. Overwhelmed, Thomas exclaims: "My Lord, my
God!" According to the Gospels, no other apostle had yet
gone so far as to call Jesus purely and simply, "God."

Thomas' doubts and objections proved every time to
be a blessing for us. To Christ's affirmation at the Last
Supper: "You know the way where I am going," Thomas
replied: "Lord, we do not know where you are going;
how can we know the way?" His observation gave Christ
the occasion to pronounce one of the most sublime sen-
tences of the whole Gospel: "I am the way, and the truth,
and the life" (Jn 14:4–6). "Thomas' incredulity," wrote
Gregory the Great, "was more useful for us than the faith
of the believing disciples."[58] By so doing, he constrained
Jesus, so to speak, to give us a "tangible" proof of the

---

58. St. Gregory the Great, *Homilies on the Gospel,* 26, 7ff. (PL 76,
1, 201ff.).

truth of his resurrection. Faith in the resurrection bene-
fited from his doubts.

There is a profound analogy between Thomas' situation and that of the believer. In every Eucharist, it is as if
Jesus entered again, "the doors being shut," into the place
of celebration (he comes from the inside, not from the outside, sacramentally, not by delivery!). In Communion, not
only does he permit us to penetrate his side, he penetrates
ours. He asks us to touch his wounds, but we can also ask
him to touch ours—wounds that are different than his, the
product of sin, not of love—and to heal them. We can relive the experience of the leper who cried out to Jesus:
"Lord, if you will, you can make me clean," and to whom,
touching him, Jesus responded: "I will; be clean!" (Mt
8:2–3).

As in the case of the good thief, here also there is dis-
creet reference to the "something more" that is required of
the believer now as then. The good thief did not see the divinity, but at least he saw the humanity; in the Eucharist not
even this is seen. Thomas believed because he saw the
wounds; we are asked to believe without having seen them.

2. The Eucharist and the Lord's Day

The theological truth on which this stanza sheds light is
that in the Eucharist not only is the crucified present but
also the risen Christ; that, as the old Roman Canon says,
it is the memorial "of the blessed passion as well as of the
resurrection from the dead." In his encyclical *Ecclesia de
Eucharistia,* John Paul II says:

> The Eucharistic Sacrifice makes present not only the
> mystery of the Savior's passion and death, but also the

mystery of the resurrection which crowned his sacrifice. It is as the living and risen One that Christ can become in the Eucharist the "bread of life" (Jn 6:35:48), the "living bread" (Jn 6:51).[59]

In every Mass, Jesus is at once victim and priest. If as victim he renders present his death, as priest he renders present his resurrection. In fact, the High Priest who speaks and says: "Take, this is my body," cannot be a dead, but a living person.

Through the resurrection, it is God the Father who enters as the protagonist of the Eucharistic mystery. If, in fact, the death of Christ is the work of humanity, the resurrection is the work of the Father. "You crucified and killed.... God raised him up," Peter cries on the day of Pentecost (see Acts 2:23ff.).

An ancient writer sheds light on the profound similarity between what occurred in the resurrection and what occurs in the Eucharist: there, the Father, through his Spirit, gave life to Christ's body lying in the sepulcher; here, with the same Spirit, he gives life to the bread and transforms it into his Son's body:

> In virtue of the liturgical action, our Lord is as it were raised from the dead.... It is similar to what occurred when the physical body of Christ received the Holy Spirit and his unction. With the coming of the Holy Spirit, the bread and wine receive an unction of grace and we believe it to be the body and blood of Christ, immortal, incorruptible, impassible, and immutable by nature, like the body of Christ itself in the resurrection.[60]

---

59. *Ecclesia de Eucharistia*, no. 14.

60. Theodore of Mopsuestia, *Catechetical Homilies*, XVI, 11ff. (Studi e Testi 145, Città del Vaticano, 1949, p. 551ff.).

The profound theological connection between the Eucharist and the resurrection creates the liturgical bond between the Eucharist and Sunday.[61] It is significant that the day par excellence (and, in the beginning, the only one) of the Eucharistic celebration is not Friday, the day of Christ's death, but Sunday, the day of his resurrection. Christ's first appearance in the Cenacle took place on the very day of the resurrection, "the first after the Sabbath"; the second appearance took place "eight days later," that is, again on the first day after the Sabbath. The emphasis on the chronological data of these two appearances shows the evangelist's intention to present Jesus' meeting with his own in the Cenacle as the prototype of the Church's Sunday assembly. At every Mass Jesus makes himself present among his disciples; he gives them peace and the Holy Spirit; in Communion, they touch, in fact receive, his wounded and risen body and, reciting the Credo, like Thomas they proclaim their faith in him. Almost all the elements of the Mass are there.

The designation "first day of the week" was very soon replaced by "the Lord's day" *(kyriaké hemera)* (Rev 1:10). The exact Latin equivalent is *dies dominica.* From being an adjective, *dominica* soon became a noun that is preserved in all the languages derived from Latin (Italian, *Domenica;* French, *Dimanche;* Spanish, *domingo*). On the contrary, the Anglo-Saxon languages retained the old pagan name *dies solis,* Sun-day (German, *Sonntag*). The bond of Sunday with Christ's resurrection is inherent in its very name; it is, in fact, thanks to the resurrection that

---

61. Cf. H. Dumaine, art. *Dimanche* in DACL, 4, Paris 1920, col. 858–994; W. Rordorf, *Sabbat und Sonntag in der Alten Kirche* (Traditio Christiana, 2) Zurich 1972; for spiritual contents, J. Gaillard, art. *Dimanche,* in *Dic. Spir.* 3 (1957), col. 948–982.

Christ was constituted *Dominus, Kyrios,* that is, Lord (cf. Rom 1:3; Acts 2:36).

Before the Judeo-Christian communities' definitive break with the synagogue, there was a sort of coexistence between the Hebrew Sabbath and the Christian Sunday; the disciples observed both. It is probable that the structure of the Mass itself, with the liturgy of the Word preceding Eucharistic liturgy, stems from this fact. Christians continued to attend the synagogue to hear the Word; they would then separate from their fellow countrymen who did not share faith in Christ and would meet separately to celebrate the Eucharist (Acts 2:46). The latter continued to present the synagogal rite unchanged, with the addition of a few expressions here and there, such as: "Jesus Christ your servant," and the words of consecration. It is the stage documented closely by the *Didaché.*

With the passing of time, Christians began to gather on their own also for the traditional liturgy, no longer going to the synagogue. In this way, the small nucleus of prayers and rites, known as *Beraka,* was enriched by what today we call the liturgy of the Word. In it, before the existence of what St. Justin calls "the memories of the apostles,"[62] that is, Christian writings, were used the same readings, prayers, and songs of praise of the synagogal liturgy with, however, an ever more markedly Christian interpretation.

In the passage of the primitive Judeo-Christian communities from Palestine to the Hellenistic communities, the situation changed rapidly. Not only was the Christian Sunday no longer regarded as the natural derivative of the Hebrew Sabbath, but the two institutions were contrast-

---

62. St. Justin, *I Apologia,* 67.

ed as Law and Gospel. For the martyr, St. Ignatius of Antioch, at the beginning of the second century, "to observe the Sabbath" or "to observe Sunday" was equivalent to living as Jews or living as Christians.[63]

Some authors had a less radical view and described the relationship between Sunday and the Hebrew Sabbath as that between figure and reality. Sunday, they say, realizes on the spiritual plane that "resting" of God and man of which the ancient Sabbath was the figure and promise. In every case, absent from the Christian Sunday was the principal meaning of the Hebrew Sabbath, that is, resting from work. Under the persecutions of the first three centuries, Sunday was a day of meeting and worship for Christians, but not of abstention from work.

Worship itself was carried out in a hidden way, in the morning before the cock crowed, to avoid arrest, and then, together with others, to attend to the usual activities of the day.[64] It was only with Constantine, in the fourth century, that the Christian Sunday was declared a feast day even for civil affairs and assumed the character of a day of rest, thereby replacing the Jewish Sabbath completely.[65] Sunday, therefore, is an apostolic institution insofar as it is a day of worship and meeting, but not as a day of rest and abstention from work.

3. The Eucharist, the Weekly Easter

Let us take a look at the contents and features of Sunday. An historical circumstance favored the birth and devel-

---

63. St. Ignatius of Antioch, *Ad. Magn.* 9, 1.

64. Cf. Pliny the Younger, *Letter to Traian*, 10, 97.

65. Cf. Eusebius of Caesarea, *Life of Constantine*, IV, 18–20 (GCS 7, 1902).

opment of the idea of Sunday as a "weekly Easter," or "little Easter," as it is sometimes called in the Eastern Churches. From the beginning, Christians were concerned to distinguish their Easter from the Hebrew Passover. Differences between Hebrews and Christians in determining the date of Passover sharpened these concerns in the fourth century, and a way of resolving the problem seemed to accentuate the importance of the weekly as opposed to the annual Easter. Eusebius of Caesarea writes:

> Moses' followers sacrificed the paschal lamb only once a year, the fourteenth of the first month, in the evening. We, instead, men of the New Testament, celebrating our Easter every Sunday, satiate ourselves continually with the Savior's body and communicate constantly with the blood of the Lamb.... Therefore, every week we celebrate our Easter, on the sacred day of the Lord.[66]

Joy was a distinctive trait of Sunday in the age of the Fathers. We see it anticipated already in the Johannine account of Christ's appearance on Easter evening: "The disciples were glad when they saw the Lord" (Jn 20:20). "We," writes Pseudo-Barnabas, "spend this eighth day in joy, this day on which Jesus rose and, after having manifested himself, ascended to heaven."[67] To Sunday is applied by extension the verse of the psalm that Jews and Christians related to Easter: "This is the day which the Lord has made; let us rejoice and be glad in it" (Ps 18:24). An institutional sign of this joy is the prohibition, derived from the apostles, of fasting, kneeling down, or exhibiting

---

66. Eusebius of Caesarea, *De solemnitate paschali*, 7 (PG 24, 701).
67. *Letter of Barnabas*, 15, 19.

other signs of penance on a Sunday, as on the days of Easter and Pentecost.[68]

Another trait that characterized the theology of Sunday in the first centuries is the topic of the eighth day, "the most fruitful source of the spirituality of Sunday at the time of the Fathers."[69] The most profound reflection on this is found in three Cappadocian Fathers, St. Basil, St. Gregory of Nazianzus, and St. Gregory of Nyssa. Sunday becomes the point of departure for a "theology of time."[70] The eighth day represents eternity that succeeds the week, which is temporal life. Being at the same time the first and the eighth day, wrote St. Basil, "Sunday is, in a certain sense, the image of the future world." "Recalling to mind eternal life, it invites us not to neglect the means that lead to it."[71] As memory and prophecy at the same time, Sunday keeps alive the memory of Easter and the eschatological expectation.

The heart of Sunday is naturally the liturgical assembly. In the description of it made by St. Justin around the middle of the second century, one can easily recognize the fundamental structure of the present Mass.[72] Concern for the poor, the imprisoned, and the sick has particular importance as an integral part of the Eucharistic celebration. St. Paul's teaching on the inseparability between Communion with the Eucharistic body of Christ and brotherly communion (1 Cor 11:17–34) did not fall on deaf ears.

---

68. Cf. Tertullian, *De corona*, 3; numerous texts in Dumaine, art. cit., col. 959–960, and in Rordorf, pp. 102 and 204.

69. Gaillard, art. *Dimanche*, in *Dic. Spir.*, 3 (1957), col. 958.

70. Cf. Several authors, *Le Huitième jour*, VS, 76, 1947; J. Daniélou, *Bible et Liturgie*, Paris 1951.

71. St. Basil the Great, *On the Holy Spirit*, 27 (PG 32, 192).

72. St. Justin, *I Apology*, 67.

What the Sunday celebration of the Eucharist represented for Christians at the time of the persecutions is shown in a moving way in the acts of the North African martyrs Saturninus and companions, who died under the Diocletian persecution in A.D. 305.[73] They were the first martyrs of the Eucharist. Their words and example might constitute a strong call and the starting point for an examination of conscience for us modern Christians. To the Roman judge who accused them of having transgressed the emperor's order not to hold meetings and hand out the Scriptures, the martyrs responded one after the other: "A Christian cannot live without the Eucharist and the Eucharist without the Christian. Don't you know that the Christian exists for the Eucharist and the Eucharist for the Christian?" "Yes, I participated with the brothers in the meeting, I celebrated the mysteries of the Lord, and I have with me, written in my heart, the divine Scriptures.... The Eucharist is the hope and salvation of Christians."[74]

4. Sunday, Law or Grace?

Moving from the Patristic to the Medieval Age, besides some positive enrichments, such as the remembrance and

---

73. *Acta ss. Saturnini et sociorum martyrum* (ca. 304), 9, 11 (ed. P. T. Ruinart, *Acta martyrum,* 1859). A phrase of these acts: *"Sine dominico non possumus,"* is sometimes translated: "We cannot live without Sunday." A suggestive translation, but unfortunately inexact. The neuter noun *dominicum* indicates the "celebration of the Lord's mysteries," "the Lord's banquet," namely the Eucharist. It is the translation of the *kyriakon (deipnon),* "the Lord's supper," of 1 Cor 11:20. The term recurs with such meaning in the African writers of the time: Tertullian, *Ad uxorem,* 2, 4; Cyprian, *De opere et eleemosynis,* 15. The accent is therefore on the Eucharist, not on Sunday; the latter is included indirectly, inasmuch as the Lord's Supper was celebrated as a rule, and for a certain period exclusively, on Sunday. The complete meaning of *dominicum* is, therefore, that of "Sunday celebration of the Lord's Supper."

74. *Acta,* 10–13.

confession of the Trinity, which became a fixed element of the Sunday liturgy (the Symbol *Quicunque,* the fixed preface of the Trinity), we observe a notable obfuscation of the pillars of Sunday spirituality in the Fathers.[75]

This development had two main factors. The first resulted from the tendency to give many Sundays their own characterization and a different name (generally taken from the first words of the entrance antiphon of the Mass), as well as the practice of frequently replacing the Sunday celebration with that of saints and other feasts. Even before this, the development of the liturgical year, absent during the first three centuries, could not fail to have consequences for the characteristic feature of Sunday. For example, how to preserve in the Sundays of Advent, which prepare for the birth of Christ, the same explicit reference to Easter, which recalls his death?

The same evolution is noted in the East. Here also, many Sundays receive their own characterization, suggested by the person or episode recalled in the Gospel passage, or by events from the history of the Church (Sunday of the Pharisee and the publican, of Orthodoxy, of the Holy Fathers of Nicea, etc.). However, the reference to Easter remains here more operative than in the West, thanks to the tropes *(anastasima)* that are sung at Vespers and to the formulas of invocation to the risen Lord during the divine liturgy.

The other negative factor was the even more accentuated tendency to equate Sunday and the day of rest, namely, the ancient Hebrew Sabbath. The debate about Sunday rest, with its emphasis on what was and was not permitted on such a day, eventually took center stage,

---

75. Cf. Galliard, col. 961 ff.

sometimes leading to the same difficulties as those surrounding Sabbath observance at the time of Christ. Sunday tended to pass from the realm of liturgy and mystery to morality, from the realm of grace to law.[76] The commandment, "remember to keep the Lord's day holy," prevailed over the joyful remembrance of the resurrection.

The rediscovery of the paschal character of Sunday was ushered in by the liturgical movement, recommended in the Second Vatican Council's Constitution on the Sacred Liturgy, and found its most mature expression in John Paul II's Apostolic Letter *Dies Domini*, of May 31, 1998, which is a little theological and pastoral "Summa" on the Lord's day.

At present the question is to live this renewed vision of Sunday. So far, progress has been made, but perhaps it is still too little. If every Mass, on its own and before all else, proclaims the Lord's *death* (1 Cor 11:26), Sunday Mass, because of the day of the week on which it is celebrated and the atmosphere that reigns there, must proclaim above all the Lord's *resurrection.* There are urgent pastoral reasons that call for a rediscovery of Sunday as the "day of the resurrection." We are now closer to the situation of the first centuries than to that of the Medieval Age. There is no longer civil legislation that, so to speak, "protects" the day of the Lord and makes it a special day. In the present organization of labor, the law of Sunday rest itself is subject to many limits and exceptions. After all, in most Christian countries these days, Saturday is also a day of rest from work.

---

76. Aquinas addresses the issue of Sunday in the part of the *Summa* dedicated to morals, speaking of the duty of Sunday rest, yet he specifies that for Christians such a commandment takes on new meaning from the resurrection of Christ: cf. *S. Th.,* II–IIae, q. 122, a. 4.

We must rediscover what Sunday was in the first centuries, when it was a special day not because of external supports, but because of its own inner force. The obligation of Sunday Mass, on its own, no longer seems sufficient to bring Christians to church on Sunday. More than the *obligation,* we must emphasize the *need* the Christian has to receive the body and blood of the Lord. "Sharing in the Eucharist should really be *the heart of Sunday* for every baptized person. It is a fundamental duty to be fulfilled not just in order to observe a precept, but as something felt as essential to a truly informed and consistent Christian life."[77]

We should present the Eucharist in such a way as to make today's Christians say what the African martyrs answered to the Roman judge: "We cannot live without the Sunday celebration of the Lord's supper!" No faithful Christian should return home from Sunday Mass without feeling that he or she, too, has been "born anew to a living hope through the resurrection of Jesus Christ from the dead" (1 Pt 1:3). Little is needed to obtain this and to place the whole Sunday celebration under the paschal sign of the resurrection: a few vibrant words at the moment of the initial greeting, or the choice of an appropriate formula for the final dismissal.

5. Do You Love Me?

After this rapid glance at the historical evolution of Sunday, let us return to our hymn to gather the prayerful conclusion of the present stanza. From the remembrance of Thomas the Apostle and of Christ's words: "Blessed are

---

77. John Paul II, *Novo Millennio Ineunte,* no. 36.

those who have not seen and yet believe!" (Jn 20:29), arises the invocation: *"Fac me tibi semper magis crédere, in te spem habére, te dilígere,"* ("That I may believe ever more, that I may ever more hope and love you"). In practice we are requesting an increase of the three theological virtues of faith, hope, and charity. These cannot but be rekindled in contact with him who is their author and object, Jesus, Son of God, who is himself God.

The prayer for an increase of faith re-echoes a similar request made by the apostles: "Lord, increase our faith!" (cf. Lk 17:5), and even more the humble request of the father of the cured epileptic: "I believe; help my unbelief!" (Mk 9:24). In the *Adoro Te Devote* the invocation is always connected to the mystery evoked in the stanza. Therefore, it is not a question in this case of faith in general, but of faith in the resurrection of Christ, which is the qualifying reality of the Christian faith. "It is no great thing to believe that Jesus died; even pagans, Jews, and evildoers all believe this. But the really great thing is to believe that he is risen. The faith of Christians is the resurrection of Christ."[78]

We have already considered the Eucharist in relation to faith, commenting on the cry, "I believe all the Son of God has said" in the second stanza and, when commenting on the last stanza, we will have occasion to meditate on the Eucharist in relation to hope. Let us reflect, therefore, on charity, the queen of the theological virtues. St. Augustine describes the Eucharist as "sign of unity and bond of charity"[79]; St. Thomas Aquinas says that it is "the sacrament of charity, its figure and source."[80] In the same

---

78. Augustine, *On the Psalms,* 120, 6 (CCL 40, p. 1,791).
79. Augustine, *On the Gospel of John,* 26, 13.
80. Aquinas, *S.Th.,* III, q. 78, a. 3, ad. 6.

vein, the Council of Trent affirmed: "At the moment of leaving the world to return to the Father, our Savior instituted this sacrament in which he lavished the riches of his love for men."[81]

The love of which the Eucharist is the sacrament refers in general to brotherly love, to the communion and unity that the Eucharist creates among those who share the same bread (cf. 1 Cor 11:15–17). Following St. Augustine's thought, this mutual charity was called the *"res sacramenti,"* namely the fruit or principal effect of the Eucharist considered as "the sacrament in which the Church is structured in time."[82] We noted that the Council of Trent sees in it God's love for men.

None of this is found in our hymn. In line with the wholly interior and personal piety of the *Adoro Te Devote,* it speaks to us of another love: the soul's love for Jesus. *Fac me...te diligere:* make me love you. It is of this love as response that an increase is requested. A call that is all the more precious for us today, so that we do not "depersonalize" the Eucharist, reducing it only to the objective dimension of community. A true communion between two free persons can only be realized in love.

The author of the *Adoro Te Devote* has chosen the episode and person of St. Thomas the Apostle to shed light on the connection between the Eucharist and Christ's resurrection. We can continue along this line by identifying ourselves with other moments and characters of the resurrection, above all with Peter. Three times the risen Christ asks him: "Do you love me?" (Jn 21:15–17). "In questioning Peter," St. Augustine writes, "Christ was

---

81. Denzinger-Schönmetzer, 1,636.
82. Augustine, *Contra Faustum*, 12, 20 (PL 42, 265).

questioning each one of us."[83] If we believe that the Jesus
we receive is the risen, living Jesus, really present as he
was then before Peter, it will not be difficult to relive this
moment intensely and also to say with Peter's humility:
"Lord, you know everything about me; you know that I
love you."

All souls that strive to live an intense Eucharistic life
have the painful experience of their own absolute inca-
pacity to receive Christ as they desire at the moment of
Communion. He is the fire, they feel like ice; he is love,
they are non-love. One day Blessed Angela of Foligno
heard Christ's voice saying to her: "My love for you has
not been a joke...I have not kept myself at a distance, but
have always felt you close to me." These words pierced
her heart like a sword because they made her clearly understand that, compared to his love, her love for him was,
precisely, "just a joke."[84]

In these circumstances, at times one feels like crying
out to Jesus as did Peter: "Depart from me, for I am a sinful man, O Lord" (Lk 5:8). Faith offers us the means to
bridge the gap. In every Communion, we can pray to the
Holy Spirit to come and to receive in us that body which
he himself formed miraculously in the Virgin's womb and
made present on the altar. "It is the Spirit of the Lord,"
says St. Francis of Assisi, "that lives in its faithful, that receives the body and blood of the Lord."[85] "We," writes
St. Paul, "have received the Spirit which is from God, that
we might understand the gifts bestowed on us by God"

---

83. Augustine, *Sermo Guelf,* 16 (PLS 2, 580).

84. Bl. Angela of Foligno, *Complete Works,* trans. P. Lachance (New
York: Paulist Press, 1993), p. 280ff.

85. Francis of Assisi, *The Admonition,* I (*Early Documents,* I,
p. 129).

(1 Cor 2:12). And when is this Spirit more necessary for us than at the moment *when God "gives" us what is most precious to him, his own Son?*

We can implore the Paraclete very simply like this: "Holy Spirit, come to help me in my weakness, because I do not know how to pray, I know not how to receive Christ" (cf. Rom 8:26). The Paraclete is the personal love of the Father for the Son; wherever he rests, a love for Jesus blossoms, which is the only love worthy of him, being a divine and not a human love, the same, identical love with which the Father loves him from all eternity.

In the second place, we can appeal to the dogma of the Communion of Saints. There are young women who, unable to afford to have a new wedding gown made for their weddings, ask some well-off married relative or acquaintance to lend her wedding gown, or they adjust their mother's wedding gown. Mary, our Mother, has the most beautiful wedding gown and is happy to lend it to whoever asks her for it to meet her Son Jesus! Metaphors aside, she is ready to give us some of her love for her Son: a simple love, without a trace of mixed motives, not made up of words, but of the whole being, as is the love of every mother for her son. Coming to us, Jesus will then not have to say: "Friend, how did you get in here without a wedding garment?" (Mt 22:12).

The saints can also encourage us in this. To recall a saint at Mass means not only to remember and invoke him or her; it means to establish a communion with him or her, to prepare to receive Jesus in his or her company, to share in the gift for which he or she is remembered by the Church, above all his or her love for Christ and the Eucharist. What is important is not to see the saints, at this moment, so much as models to imitate as powerful friends of which "to make use."

Love for Jesus is sung in a wonderful way in the twelfth-century hymn attributed to St. Bernard and inserted, in part, into the Liturgy of the Hours: *Iesu Dulcis Memoria.* Let us select some stanzas from it; they can give wings to our thanksgiving at Communion. Christ rejoices on hearing it because in these words he feels once again the ardent charity and emotion with which so many saints and souls in love (the *experts!*), repeated it to him before us, with tears in their eyes.

> *Iesu, dulcis memoria,*
> *dans vera cordis gaudia,*
> *sed super mel et omnia,*
> *eius dulcis praesentia.*

> *Nec lingua valet dicere,*
> *nec littera exprimere:*
> *expertus potest credere,*
> *quid sit Iesum diligere.*

> Jesus, the very thought of Thee
> With sweetness fills the breast!
> Yet sweeter far Thy face to see
> And in Thy presence rest.

> But what to those who find? Ah! this
> Nor tongue nor pen can show
> The love of Jesus, what it is,
> None but his loved ones know.

V.

O Thou Memorial of Our Lord's Own Dying!

The Eucharist: Presence of the Incarnation and Memorial of Easter

1. Sacrifice and Banquet

O memoriále mortis Dómini,
Panis vivus vitam praestans hómini,
praesta meae menti de te vívere,
et te illi semper dulce sápere.

O thou Memorial of our Lord's own dying!
O Bread that living art and vivifying!
Make ever Thou my soul on Thee to live;
ever a taste of Heavenly sweetness give.

The fifth stanza of the *Adoro Te Devote* is, theologically, the most profound of the whole hymn. In four brief verses the author summarizes the essence of the Eucharistic vision of St. Paul and St. John. The Eucharist as "memorial of the Lord's death" is the feature that characterizes the Pauline tradition (cf. 1 Cor 11:24; Lk 22:19); the

Eucharist as "living bread" characterizes the Johannine vision (cf. Jn 6:30ff).[86]

The Pauline perspective emphasizes the idea of sacrifice and immolation, making the Eucharist the proclamation of the Lord's death and the fulfillment of Easter: "For as often as you eat this bread and drink the cup, you proclaim the Lord's death" (1 Cor 11:26), and, "Christ, our paschal lamb, has been sacrificed" (1 Cor 5:7). The Johannine perspective emphasizes the idea of the Eucharist as banquet and communion: "My flesh is food indeed, and my blood is drink indeed" (Jn 6:55). One explains the Eucharist starting from the paschal mystery, the other, from the Incarnation. If, in fact, the flesh of Christ gives life to the world, it is because "the Word became flesh" (Jn 1:14).

The two dimensions of the Eucharist, as sacrament and sacrifice, are reconciled, something not always easy to keep together. A synthesis which is very close to our hymn's is the antiphon, *O sacrum convivium:* "O sacred banquet in which we nourish ourselves on Christ, the memorial of his passion is celebrated, the soul is filled with grace, and we are given the pledge of future glory." But the true synthesis of the two dimensions is the Mass itself: with the consecration it makes the sacrifice present, and with Communion it realizes the banquet.

From this we see how much the Eucharist is impoverished by making one aspect absolute to the exclusion of the others. There were periods when the faithful's attention was wholly concentrated on the consecration, on the

---

86. The expression, "living bread that gives life" *(panis vivus vitam praestans)* corresponds to the "living and vital bread" *(panis vivus et vitalis)* of the other well-known Eucharistic hymn, *Lauda Sion.*

Mass as sacrifice for the living and the dead, with general abstention from Communion. It would be equally serious to emphasize today only the aspect of the banquet, neglecting that of sacrifice. This is the danger that Pope John Paul II warns against in the encyclical *Ecclesia de Eucharistia* when he writes: "At times one encounters an extremely reductive understanding of the Eucharistic mystery. Stripped of its sacrificial meaning, it is celebrated as if it were simply a fraternal banquet."[87]

2. The Bread That Gives Life

Since antiquity, the two visions of the Eucharist—the Pauline centered on the paschal mystery, and the Johannine centered on the Incarnation of the Word—have given rise to two different but complementary Eucharistic theologies and spiritualities: the Alexandrian and the Antiochene. If we wish to explore today the riches contained in both visions, there is no better way than to appropriate the results of that very rich period of Christian thought. Moreover, the two conceptions did not come to an end with the two schools that elaborated them, but are present and recognizable in the whole of subsequent tradition, as two sorts of archetypes of Eucharistic piety.

We will begin with the Alexandrian vision, famously inspired by Johannine Christology. It is clear from the outset how closely connected it is to a certain way of understanding the Incarnation:

> And the Word was made flesh: it did not say that he was made in the flesh but, repeatedly, that he was made flesh, to show the union.... Therefore, whoever

---

87. *Ecclesia de Eucharistia,* no. 10.

eats Christ's holy flesh has eternal life: in fact, the flesh
has in itself the Word that is Life by nature.

The Eucharist, the same text continues, is the seed of
immortality sown in us that, in the end, will make us rise
from death:

> We will rise because Christ is in us, through his own
> flesh; indeed, it is impossible that Life not vivify those
> in which it is found. Just as, when kindling a spark of
> fire, we put it in straw so as to preserve the source of
> the fire; so also, Our Lord Jesus Christ has hidden life
> within us through his flesh, and has inserted it as the
> seed of immortality which frees us from all corruption
> that is now in us.[88]

While awaiting the final resurrection, the Eucharist
exercises a *power of healing* in whoever receives it:

> It has the force to drive out not only death but also our
> weakness. In fact, Christ dwelling in us mitigates the
> law of the flesh that rages in our members, stimulates
> piety toward God, mortifies temptations, not imputing
> to us the sins into which we have fallen, but rather cur-
> ing us as sick persons.[89]

Everything here assumes an extremely concrete and
realistic character. Whoever eats the body and drinks the
blood of Christ finds himself "united and merged with
him, as wax united to wax." As leaven makes the whole
dough ferment, so a small portion of Eucharistic bread
fills our whole body with divine energy. He is in us and
we in him, as the leaven is in the dough and the dough in

---

88. St. Cyril of Alexandria, *On the Gospel of John*, IV, 2 (PG 73, 581).
89. Ibid., IV, 2 (PG 73, 585).

the leaven.[90] Only when read with these premises can one fully appreciate the profundity of Jesus' word that inspires all of this vision of the Eucharist: "As the living Father sent me, and I live because of the Father, so he who eats me will live because of me" (Jn 6:58).[91]

The practical consequence of all of this is an urgent exhortation to frequent Communion, which is why St. Cyril's authority is often invoked later against the Jansenists. Some, he notes, appeal to the words of St. Paul, who states that whoever eats the body of Christ unworthily is guilty of profaning it; but the conclusion to draw from this is not to abstain from frequent Communion, but to purify oneself as soon as possible to be able to receive it. "How, in fact, will you become worthy if not precisely by approaching Christ's holiness?"[92]

Suffice it to read Cabasilas' *Life in Christ* to realize how far this vision of the Eucharist has shaped the subsequent spirituality of the Orthodox Church. Almost all the terms we have been considering are found there and inserted in a wonderful synthesis of mystical spirituality. With a bold use of the "interchange of properties" *(communicatio idiomatum)* typical of this tradition, the Eucharist is called "the body of God."[93] Cabasilas writes:

> Christ flows into us and unites with us, but changes us and transforms us into himself as a drop of water poured in an infinite ocean of perfumed ointment. Such are the effects that this ointment can produce in those who encounter him: not only does he render them sim-

---

90. Ibid. (PG 73, 584).
91. Ibid., IV, 3 (PG 73, 585ff.).
92. Ibid., IV, 2 (PG 73, 584ff.).
93. Nicholas Cabasilas, *Life in Christ,* IV, 3 (PG 150, 593).

ply perfumed, and make them breathe that perfume, but he transforms their very substance into that ointment's perfume.[94]

For those who celebrate Mass or receive Communion every day, this Eucharistic doctrine can help them not to live all this as a mere devotional practice—relying on the infinite value of every Mass or other such considerations—but rather as a vital need of the soul.

Because we bear this treasure in earthen vessels, and corrupt matter does not permit the seal to remain unaltered, we do not limit ourselves to tasting the medicine only once; rather, we taste it uninterruptedly. A potter must always be alongside his clay, constantly repairing the molded shape. In the same way, we should draw continuous benefit from the doctor's hand, so that he restores the crumbling material and straightens our yielding will, in case death should come and catch us unawares.[95]

This Eucharistic doctrine was formed at a time when all theological concern was concentrated on the figure of Christ and the unity of his person. We can see the value of other elements in the Johannine vision, which in the meantime have acquired great topical interest. One of them is the emphasis on service, which makes the evangelist place the washing of the feet where the Synoptics place the institution of the Supper; another is the highlighting of the Father's role in the Eucharist: "It was not Moses who gave you the bread from heaven; my Father gives you the true bread from heaven," says Jesus to the Jews (Jn 6:32).

---

94. Ibid.
95. Ibid. (PG 150, 596).

The Eucharist is the Father's gift to the world. The mystery contained in the words: "God so loved the world that he gave his only Son" (Jn 3:16), is made present in every Mass. In the priest who offers us the body and blood of Christ at the moment of Communion, we can see, with the eyes of faith, the Father in person, who comes to give us "the bread of heaven, the true bread" and says: "Take, this is the body of my Only-begotten Son which I have given for you."

Not only does the Father give us the Eucharist, he also gives himself in the Eucharist. Because there is only one indivisible divine nature, in receiving the divinity of the Son we also receive the Father. "Whoever sees me sees the Father," also means "whoever receives me, receives the Father." One day (it was a Saturday of the Second Week of Lent), after listening to the Gospel passage of the parable of the Prodigal Son, I understood clearly that Communion offered me, there and then, the incredible opportunity of receiving the Father's forgiving embrace—and not only mentally!

3. The Eucharist: Memorial of Easter

We now move to the Pauline vision of the Antiochenes. It does not contradict the previous vision, but enriches and completes it. By keeping the two perspectives together, we can have a much more complete vision of the Eucharist. We see it simultaneously as the real presence of the incarnate Word and as the memorial of his passion and resurrection; the sacrament renders present to us, at the same time, the mystery of the Incarnation and the paschal mystery.

For the Antiochenes also, the Eucharist constituted the sacramental face of Christology, the place where its richness is best revealed and its insufficiency (the Nestorian tendency) least perceived. And it was natural that a conception that highlights the paschal mystery so strongly, as did that of the Antiochenes, would be translated into a particularly rich and suggestive Eucharistic doctrine. Theodore of Mopsuestia's two catecheses devoted to the Mass are among the classics of the Patristic mystical catechesis. He writes:

> In the first place, one should know that, taking this food, we participate in a *sacrifice*. It is true that with this food and with this drink we recall the death of our Lord and believe that these elements are the memory of his passion.[96]

As we see, the Eucharist is presented from the beginning in its sacrificial aspect. This concept was certainly not unknown to the Alexandrians, but here it occupies a far more prominent place. More than a *real presence of a person,* the Eucharist is regarded as a *memorial of an event,* the death-resurrection of Christ. In the Alexandrian perspective, Eucharistic Communion brings us into contact with the flesh of Christ, which has become vivifying because of the Incarnation and the hypostatic union with the Word; here, above all, it brings us into contact with the body of Christ that, according to St. Paul, has become life-giving because of the resurrection (cf. 1 Cor 15:45).

In no other ancient catechesis is the role of the Holy Spirit so emphasized as in the Antiochene. The Holy Spirit is not only he who is *given* to us by the Eucharist, but also he who *gives* us the Eucharist. It is he who, at the

---

96. Theodore of Mopsuestia, *Catechetical Homilies,* XV, 15 (*Studi e Testi* 145, Città del Vaticano, 1949, p. 485).

moment of the consecration, thanks to the epiclesis, descends into the bread and wine and renders them the living and vivifying body and blood of Christ, just as, in the resurrection, he descended into Christ's dead body and raised it to life and immortality.[97] Everything is centered on the paschal mystery:

> With the help of this memorial, of these symbols and signs, with sweetness and joy we approach Christ, risen from the dead. We embrace him, because we see him risen and we hope to participate in his resurrection.[98]

We draw near to receive the body and blood of Christ with the certainty that with them the divine energies of the resurrection are communicated to us in the forms of peace, courage, and hope.

Today, we can also complete and update this second Patristic vision of the Eucharist in the light of the Mystical Body and the universal priesthood of all the baptized. The doctrine of the Mystical Body assures us that, in the Mass, the Church is not only she who offers the sacrifice, but also she who offers herself in sacrifice together with her head. As St. Augustine said: "In what is offered, it is also herself that the Church offers."[99] In turn, the truth of the universal priesthood allows the extension of this participation to all the faithful, not only to the priests. Speaking of this "common priesthood," the Second Vatican Council's Constitution *Lumen Gentium* states:

> The faithful, in virtue of their royal priesthood, join in the offering of the Eucharist.... Taking part in the

---

97. Ibid., XVI, 12 (p. 553): see text quoted, chap. 4, n. 60.
98. Ibid., XVI, 26 (p. 575).
99. Augustine, *On the City of God*, X, 6 (CCL 47, 279).

Eucharistic sacrifice, which is the fount and apex of the whole Christian life, they offer the Divine Victim to God, and offer themselves along with It. Thus both by reason of the offering and through Holy Communion all take part in this liturgical service, not indeed, all in the same way, but each in that way which is proper to himself.[100]

The Eucharist, therefore, is the act of the whole people of God, not only in the passive sense, which redounds to the benefit of all, but also actively, in the sense that it is accomplished with the participation of all. Commenting on Romans 12:1 ("I appeal to you therefore, brethren, by the mercies of God, to present your bodies as a living sacrifice, holy and acceptable to God, which is your spiritual worship"), St. Peter Chrysologus said:

Thus the Apostle sees all men raised to the priestly dignity to offer their own bodies as a living sacrifice. O immense dignity of the Christian priesthood! Man has become victim and priest in his own right. He no longer seeks outside himself that which he must immolate to God, but carries with himself and in himself that which he sacrifices to God.... Brothers, this sacrifice is modeled on that of Christ...therefore, O man, be the sacrifice and the priest of God.[101]

Jesus explained the things of the Kingdom in parables; let us adopt his method and seek to understand, with the help of a modern parable, what happens in the Eucharistic celebration. There was an employee in a large firm who admired and loved the general manager im-

---

100. *Lumen Gentium*, 10–11.
101. St. Peter Chrysologus, *Sermo* 108 (PL 52, 499ff.).

mensely. He wanted to give him a present for his birthday. Before presenting it, however, he asked all of his colleagues to sign the gift. And so, when the manager received it, it was the joint tribute of all his employees and a sign of the esteem and love of them all, although only one of them had paid the price.

Is not this exactly what happens in the Eucharistic sacrifice? Jesus admires and loves the heavenly Father boundlessly. Each day, until the end of the world, he wishes to give him the most precious gift imaginable—the gift of his own life. In the Mass, he invites all his "brothers" to sign the gift, so that it reaches God the Father as the joint gift of all his children, "my sacrifice and yours," as the priest says in the *Orate fratres*. However, in reality, we know that only one has paid the price—and what a price!

Our signatures are the few drops of water that are mixed with the wine in the chalice; our signatures are, above all, that solemn "Amen" which the liturgy has the whole assembly pronounce at the end of the Eucharistic Prayer: "Through him, with him, in him, in the unity of the Holy Spirit, all glory and honor are yours, Almighty Father, for ever and ever. Amen!"

We know that whoever has signed a commitment has the duty to honor his or her signature. This means that, as we come out of Mass, we too must make our life a gift of love to the Father and to our brothers and sisters. Thus, a Christian's whole life becomes a Eucharist, not only during the Mass.

4. He Who Eats Me Will Live Because of Me

The prayerful conclusion of the fifth stanza of the *Adoro Te Devote* is as simple as it is profound. It says literally: "Make

my soul ever live on Thee; and taste Thy sweetness constantly." The first part of the phrase is clearly inspired by
John 6:57: "As the living Father sent me, and I live because
of the Father, *so he who eats me will live because of me.*"

The preposition "because of" (in Greek, *dià*) here indicates cause and purpose; it is at once a movement between origin and destination. It means that whoever eats
the body of Christ lives "through" him, that is, because
of him, in virtue of the life that comes from him, and
lives "in view of him," that is, for his glory, his love, and
his Kingdom. As Jesus "lives on" the Father and for the
Father, so by our communing with the holy mystery of
his body and his blood we live on Jesus and for Jesus.

It is, in fact, the stronger vital principle that assimilates the weaker, not vice versa. It is the vegetable that
assimilates the mineral, not vice versa; it is the animal
that assimilates the vegetable and the mineral, not vice
versa. So too, on the spiritual plane, it is the divine that
assimilates the human, not vice versa. So that, while in
all other cases it is the eater who assimilates what he
eats, here the one who is eaten assimilates the one who
eats him. To the one who draws near to receive him,
Jesus repeats what he said to St. Augustine: "It will not
be you who assimilate me, but it will be I who assimilate you."[102]

In the Eucharist, therefore, there is not only *communion,* but also *assimilation,* between Christ and ourselves. Communion is not only the union of two bodies,
two minds, two wills, but it is also assimilation to the one
body, the one mind and will of Christ. "He who is united
to the Lord becomes one spirit with him" (1 Cor 6:17).

---

102. Cf. Augustine, *Confessions,* VII, 10.

These are classic concepts and examples. But now I would like to stress another aspect of Eucharistic Communion which is not so often talked about. The Letter to the Ephesians states that human marriage is a symbol of the union between Christ and the Church: "For this reason a man shall leave his father and mother and be joined to his wife, and the two shall become one. This is a great mystery, and I mean it in reference to Christ and the Church!" (5:31–33). Now, according to St. Paul, the immediate consequence of marriage is that the body of the husband becomes the wife's and, vice versa, the body of the wife becomes the husband's (cf. 1 Cor 7:4).

Applied to the Eucharist this means that the incarnate Word's incorruptible, life-giving flesh becomes "mine," but my flesh, my humanity, also becomes Christ's, he makes it his own. In the Eucharist we receive the body and blood of Christ, but Christ also "receives" our body and our blood! Jesus, writes St. Hilary of Poitiers, assumes the flesh of the one who assumes his.[103] He says to us: "Take, this is my body," but we can also say to him: "Take, this is my body."

In the collection of Eucharistic poems titled "Canticle of the Hidden God" (the title derives, I believe, from *latens deitas* of the *Adoro Te Devote!*), the future Pope John Paul II, Karol Wojtyla, calls this new subject, whose life was made his own by Christ, "the Eucharistic I":

Then it will happen,
the miracle of the transformation:
behold, you will become me—
the Eucharistic I.[104]

---

103. St. Hilary of Poitiers, *De Trinitate*, 8, 16 (PL 10, 248): *"Eius tantum in se adsumptam habens carnem, qui suam sumpserit."*

104. K. Wojtyla, *Tutte le opere letterarie* (Milan: Bompiani, 2000), p. 75.

There is nothing of my life that does not belong to Christ. No one should say: "Ah, Jesus does not know what it means to be married, to be a woman, to have lost a child, to be sick, to be elderly, to be a person of color!" If you know it, so does he, thanks to you and in you. What Christ did not experience "according to the flesh"— since his earthly existence, like that of all humanity, was limited to some experiences—he now lives and "experiences" as risen "according to the Spirit," thanks to the spousal Communion of the Mass. All that "was lacking" to the full "Incarnation" of the Word is "completed" in the Eucharist. Blessed Elizabeth of the Trinity understood the profound reason for this when she wrote: "The bride belongs to the groom. Mine has taken me. He wants me to be an additional humanity for him."[105]

In the liturgy of the Mass prior to its reform, before beginning the Offertory, the priest turned to the people with the greeting, *Dominus vobiscum* (the Lord be with you). Here is what the poet Claudel read into those words and the priest's imploring look:

> The Lord is with you, my brothers! My brothers,
>   did you hear me?
> My little flock, it is not only the paten, it is not only
>   the chalice with the wine,
> it is you—the whole of you—that I would like to hold
>   and raise in my hands...
> See, the collection plate is coming round. Have you
>   nothing else to give,
> except that miserable farthing? ...
> Nothing other than your purse to open?
> Is there no one here suffering? ...

---

105. Bl. Elizabeth of the Trinity, *Letter* 261, to her mother.

No one afflicted among you? Really? No sin and
    no pain?
No mother who has lost her child? Has no one here
    failed without it being their fault?
[I add: No priest, no man or woman religious who
    has failed through no fault of their own, or even
    through their own fault?]
No young girl abandoned by her fiancé because her
    brother has squandered her dowry?
No sick person who has been diagnosed by his doctor
    and who knows there is no hope?
Why then deprive your God of that which is his own?
Your tears and your faith, your blood with his in
    the chalice!
Like the wine and bread, this is the material of his
    sacrifice!
This is what ransoms the world; this is what he
    thirsts and hungers for,
these tears, like coins thrown into the fountain, oh my
    God, so many sufferings in vain!
Have pity on him who had only thirty-three years
    to suffer!
Unite your passion to his, as one can only die once![106]

What endless reason for wonder and consolation is
the thought that our humanity becomes Christ's humanity! But also, what responsibility comes from all of
this! If my eyes have become Christ's eyes, my mouth
that of Christ, what greater reason could there be for not
allowing my eyes to look at lustful images, my tongue to
speak ill of my brother or sister, my body to serve as an
instrument of sin? "Shall I therefore take the members

---

106. P. Claudel, *La Messe là-bas*, in *Oeuvre poétique* (Paris: Gallimard, 1967), pp. 502–503.

of Christ and make them members of a prostitute?"
(1 Cor 6:15)

5. The "Wonderful Exchange"

Giving to Jesus what is ours—troubles, pains, failures,
and sins—is, however, only the first act. In Communion,
we must immediately pass from *giving* to *receiving*. We
must receive Christ's holiness! Unless we go on to make
this "bold stroke," we will never understand "the enormity" of the Eucharist.

There is an act that carried out among men is a sin
and punished by the law, but when carried out with
Christ is not only allowed, but also most highly recommended: "undue appropriation." In every Communion,
Jesus "incites" us to commit an act of undue appropriation! (Undue, in the sense of not deserved, not owed,
purely gratuitous!) Where else in the believer's life will
that "wonderful exchange" *(admirabile commercium)* of
which the liturgy speaks be brought about, concretely, if
not at the moment of Communion? There we have the
possibility to give Jesus our rags and receive from him the
"robe of righteousness" (cf. Is 61:10). In fact, it is written
that "God made him our wisdom, our righteousness, our
sanctification and redemption" (1 Cor 1:30). That which
he became "for us" was destined for us, belongs to us.
"That which belongs to Christ is more ours than what is
our own."[107] When we discover this, it lends wings to our
spiritual life.

When Jacob presented himself to his father Isaac to
receive the blessing intended for his brother, Esau, the fa-

---

107. N. Cabasilas, *Vita in Christo*, IV, 6 (PG 150, 613).

ther noticed that the voice was not that of his firstborn, but the garments he wore led him to mistake Jacob for Esau, and he gave him his blessing (cf. Gen 27:1ff.). Something similar occurs when we present ourselves before the heavenly Father after having received the Eucharist. He "mistakes" us for his only-begotten Son and blesses us.

What is required of us in return for all of this? Nothing but "deep-felt gratitude." If it is sincere, it will not leave us in our spiritual inertia; it will be the incentive that will goad us into action: to embrace the cross, to welcome our brothers and sisters, to struggle against our defects, to live in constant repentance for our sins.

6. How Sweet Is Your Spirit, Lord!

The Eucharist has always been one of the privileged places of the mystical experience,[108] and it is to this stage that the *Adoro Te Devote* transports us when, at the end, it makes us ask to "taste the sweetness" of Christ in the Eucharist *(et te illi semper dulce sapere)*. There is a whole series of testimonies that associates the Eucharist and the experience of spiritual sweetness. The Latin word *sápere* has become the word "to know" in many Romance languages *(sapére, saber, savoir)*, but it means much more than knowing; it also means to savor, to relish.

We have a whole series of testimonies associating the Eucharist with an experience of spiritual sweetness. Applying to the Sacrament of the Altar the verse of the Canticle: "I eat my honeycomb and my honey, I drink my wine

---

108. Cf. E. Longprè, *Eucharistie et expérience mystique,* in *Dict. Spir.,* 4, col. 1586–1621.

and my milk" (Song 5:1), St. Ambrose comments: "See how there is no bitterness, but only sweetness in this bread?"[109] From the fifth century on, in many churches of Christendom, the song, *"Gustate et videte quoniam suavis Dominus"* (Ps 34:9), was intoned: "Taste and see how sweet the Lord is." A verse that is also proclaimed today, especially in English-speaking countries, by the priest at the moment of presenting Christ's body to the communion of the faithful.

The *Ave Verum* also ends with the exclamation: *"O Iesu dulcis, O Iesu pie, O Iesu fili Mariae!"* ("O sweet Jesus, O loving Jesus, O Jesus son of Mary!") But the text that best summarizes this theme of the Eucharist's sweetness is the antiphon for the *Magnificat* for Vespers of the feast of *Corpus Christi:* "Lord, how good you are and how gentle is your spirit! When you wished to show your children your goodness, you gave them a most sweet bread from heaven, to fill the hungry with good things and send the haughty rich away empty-handed."[110]

We end this meditation on the Eucharist-Communion uniting ourselves to the amazement of St. Thomas Aquinas (and of the French composer, Cesar Franck, who wrote one of the most well-known sacred melodies for the text) at the thought that the bread of angels has become the food of mortals:[111]

---

109. St. Ambrose, *On the Sacraments*, V, 17 (PL 16, 449).

110. *"O quam suavis est, Domine, spiritus tuus! Qui ut dulcedinem tuam in filios demonstrares, pane suavissimo de caelo praestito, esaurientes reples bonis, fastidiosos divites dimittens inanes."*

111. Hymn *Sacris sollemniis* for the office of the solemnity of *Corpus Christi*.

Panis Angelicus fit panis hominum;
dat panis coelicus figuris terminum:
O res mirabilis! Manducat Dominum
Servus, pauper et humilis.

The bread of angels becomes the bread of man;
this bread of heaven does away with symbols.
What a marvel! The poor, the servant and the
    humble
may feed on their Lord.

VI.

O Loving Pelican! Jesus Our Lord!

The Eucharist, Sacrament of Nonviolence

1. "Our Pelican"

Jesus instituted the Eucharist under the sign of bread and wine, that is, of eating and drinking, that together make up the image of a banquet and a feast. At Capernaum he said: "Unless you eat the flesh of the Son of man and drink his blood, you have no life in you," and again, "My flesh is real food, and my blood is real drink" (Jn 6:53–55). When instituting the Eucharist, he said, "Take and eat.... Take and drink of it, all of you." He did not say, "some of you," or "whoever wants to," but "all of you."

St. Paul attests to the fact that this command was faithfully carried out in the Apostolic Church by once mentioning "participation in the blood of Christ," in fact, before "participation in the body of Christ" (1 Cor 10:16). The Fathers of the Church give the same importance to Communion with the blood of Christ as they do to Communion with his body, attributing to it, in particular, the remission of sins and the gift of the Holy Spirit. "I want the bread of God that is the flesh of Christ," St. Ignatius of Antioch cried out on his way to martyrdom, "I want his blood to drink, which is incorruptible love!"[112]

By the time that the *Adoro Te Devote* was composed, many factors had already had the effect tacitly of making the Eucharist the sacrament of the body of Christ, and much less so of his blood. By this time, Communion was given under the species of bread alone to the few faithful who approached it. Moreover, the rich Eucharistic worship that was developing outside the Mass involuntarily contributed to this, having only the Host and not the chalice as its object. The blood of Christ appeared as a kind of appendage to the body of Christ.

Christian piety sought to remedy this anomaly by developing a growing devotion to the blood of Christ outside the Eucharistic mystery. Proof of this was the institution of a separate feast of the Most Precious Blood on July 1, as though the feast of the body of Christ was not also the feast of his blood. Following the Council, that feast was abolished, while the so-called feast of the "Most Holy Body of Christ" was given the more inclusive name of "Feast of the Most Holy Body and Blood of Christ."

In this light, it is positively surprising to find in the *Adoro Te Devote* a whole stanza dedicated to the blood of Christ:

> *Pie Pellicáne, Jesu Dómine,*
> *me immúndum munda tuo sánguine,*
> *cujus una stilla salvum fácere*
> *totum mundum quit ab omni scélere.*[113]

---

112. St. Ignatius of Antioch, *To the Romans*, 7, 3.

113. Instead of *totum mundum quit ab—omni scelere,* which makes for an unnatural division of the verse, Wilmart's text has *totum mundum posset—omni scelere.*

O loving Pelican! O Jesus, Lord!
Unclean I am, but cleanse me in Thy Blood;
of which a single drop, for sinners spilt,
is ransom for a world's entire guilt.

At the time our hymn was composed, Christianity was still under the strong influence of the Eucharistic miracle of Bolsena of 1263. A Bohemian priest on his way to Rome was celebrating Mass in the Basilica of St. Christina in Bolsena. In his heart he had doubts about the reality of Christ's presence; when he elevated the Host after the consecration, blood began to flow from it. The blood-stained corporal was taken to Pope Urban IV, who was in nearby Orvieto. Convinced of the miracle, the Pontiff ordered that construction begin on the famous Cathedral of Orvieto to house the relic. In the following year, 1264, he extended the feast of *Corpus Christi*, already celebrated in some churches in Belgium, to the whole Church, asking St. Thomas Aquinas to compose the Office of the feast, or at least to work out the one already existing.

The hymn's author was certainly aware of the event and perhaps drew inspiration from it in writing this stanza. The discourse on the blood of Christ is introduced by a symbol: the pelican. In ancient times and in the Middle Ages it was commonly believed that the pelican wounded its breast with its beak so as to feed its hungry young with its own blood, or to restore them to life if they were dead.[114] Piety

---

114. Augustine, *On the Psalms*, 101:8 (PL 36, 1299); Isidore of Seville, *Orig.*, 12, 7, 26; Christianus Campililiensis, *Speculum animalium*, 2, 162 (CCL, CM, 19B, 1992): *"Pellicanus subitam pullis dat sanguine vitam";* Dante Alighieri, *Paradiso*, XXV, 112–113: *"This one is he* (John) *who lay upon the breast / Of our true Pelican."*

toward its young, whether in symbol or reality, suggested to the author the adjective pious, loving *(pie Pellicane)*.

St. John Chrysostom expressed the same thought with an equally beautiful and certainly more "human" symbol: "As a woman nourishes her newborn with her own blood and milk, so Christ nourishes with his own blood those whom he himself has begotten."[115]

2. The Drop of Blood That Saves the World

In this stanza the usual order is inverted: first comes the prayerful application, "unclean I am, but cleanse me," and then the theological affirmation, "a single drop of blood is enough to save the whole world." In the commentary, however, we must follow the logical order and reflect on the truth of faith before applying it to life.

The above theological affirmation is a solemn act of faith in the universal value of the blood of Christ, "a single drop" of which, it says, "is enough to save the whole world." We find an almost identical affirmation in St. Thomas Aquinas: "The smallest drop of the blood of Christ would have sufficed to redeem mankind."[116]

Can we still share the certainty that a single drop of Christ's blood is enough to save the whole world without lacking in the esteem we owe to other religions and failing to recognize in them a certain salvific value for their

---

115. St. John Chrysostom, *Baptismal Catecheses*, III, 19 (SCh 50ff., p. 162).

116. Aquinas, *Quodlibet 2*, q. 1, a. 2, sc. 2 (*Opera omnia*, XXV, 2, ed. the Leonine Commission and ...Éditions du Cerf , 1966, p. 213): *"Minima gutta sanguinis Christi suffecisset ad redemptionem humani generis."* The expression, which St. Thomas attributes to St. Bernard, goes back in fact to Nicholas of Clairvaux (PL 144, 762) and is read in several sources of the period, indicated in a note of the cited edition of Aquinas.

own followers? Some think so and relate the elements of goodness and truth they contain to the eternal Word and the Spirit of God. As persons of the Trinity—they affirm—Word and Spirit were operating in the world before the coming of Christ and continue to operate even after his resurrection, not in dependence on the mystery of Christ, but parallel to it, in a relationship of complementarity, not subordination.

However, we must ask ourselves if in order to acknowledge that other religions have their own dignity and a certain right to exist in the divine plan of salvation, it is necessary to disconnect them from Christ's paschal mystery, or can the same result be obtained by keeping them somehow mysteriously related to it in a way "known only to God"? "A particular event limited in time and space, as Christ is, cannot exhaust the infinite potential of God and of his Word." True, but it can realize as much of that infinite potential as suffices for the salvation of the world that is itself finite!

If we believe that the blood shed on the cross is the blood of God made man, as we proclaimed earlier in the hymn ("*Deum tamen verum te confiteor*," "I acknowledge Thee as true God"), the affirmation that one single drop of his blood can save the whole world is no longer an exaggeration, but a necessity. "He is the expiation for our sins, and not for ours only but also for the sins of the whole world" (1 Jn 2:2).

3. Why the Blood?

The most topical question raised by the words of the *Adoro Te Devote* refers to the means chosen to accomplish this universal salvation. Why blood precisely? Are we to think that the sacrifice of Christ—and, therefore, the Eucharist that renews it sacramentally—only confirms the affirmation that "violence is the heart, the secret soul of the sacred"?[117]

Today we are able to shed a new and liberating light on the Eucharist by following the very same path that led the French thinker, René Girard, to move from the assertion that violence is intrinsic to the sacred to the conviction that Christ's paschal mystery has unmasked the alliance between violence and the sacred and has broken it for ever. For our purpose, we need not go into details; it is enough to recall the essential passages.[118]

Freud had explained the origin of religion in terms of the killing of the primordial father by his sons, who then sublimate the slain one, making him God-Father. Girard also thinks that at the origin of the sacred there is violence and blood, but the explanation he gives is very different. It is not just a question of the desire to have access to the mother and the women of the clan, which the father prevents, but of human desire in general. It is, by nature, mimetic; in other words, it imitates another's desire. The human being discovers what is desirable by looking at what others desire. The classic example is a child who is determined to have a toy, even if he has many others at his disposal, only because another child is interested in it.

Rivalry and violence are born from the tendency to desire the same objects (which can be things, persons, but also recognition or predominance). From this, Thomas

---

117. Cf. R. Girard, *Violence and the Sacred* (Baltimore: Johns Hopkins University Press, 1977).

118. I have drawn on a useful introduction to the subject by M. Kirwan, *Discovering Girard* (London: DLT, 2004).

Hobbes derived the "war of all against all" that character-izes human nature and from which we are saved, he says, by jointly agreeing (social contract theory) to establish a higher power, which is the State ("Leviathan"), capable of controlling violence by force.

For Girard, the crisis of violence must be resolved in another way: by transforming the aggression of all against all into "the aggression of all against one"—the well-known mechanism of the scapegoat. One element—usu-ally the weakest and most vulnerable—is chosen and singled out as responsible for the evil that afflicts the com-munity. Enemies are strangely reconciled in their common aggression toward the victim. The latter can be a member of the community or an external enemy. Typical is the case of schoolchildren where rivals become friends, sin-gling out someone weak or "different" against whom to lash out.

Here, too, Girard continues, as in the case of the slay-ing of the father, the victim—the scapegoat—is sublimat-ed and elevated to a divine state. Myth, worship, religion, and the sacred are born. It was at this point in his re-search that Girard enunciated the thesis: "Violence is the heart and secret soul of the sacred," which, according to the newspaper, Le Monde, made 1972 "a year to mark with an asterisk in the annals of humanity."

However, before that date an illness had driven the scholar to approach Christianity once more and to go back to the Bible. At Easter 1959, he spoke publicly about his "conversion," declaring himself a believer and returning to the Church after twenty-six years of estrangement. This al-lowed him to go beyond merely analyzing the mechanism of violence, a hopeless task, and to point to a way out. In a rare event among scholars of his calibre, Girard was not afraid to pronounce out loud, even in scientific circles, the name of the remedy: Jesus Christ. Many, unfortunately, continue to quote Girard as the one who denounced the alliance between violence and the sacred, but fail to mention the Girard who pointed to Christ's paschal mystery as the total and definitive break-up of such an alliance.

From his reading of the Old Testament, especially the songs of the Servant of Yahweh, Girard had already discovered the existence of a different kind of religion: a religion whose God is not an accomplice of violence, but who is on the side of the victim. But, above all, it is the historical fact of the death and resurrection of Christ that is the new element, and reveals "the things hidden since the foundation of the world."[119]

By his doctrine and life, Jesus exposed and destroyed the mechanism of the scapegoat that canonizes violence, making himself, the innocent one, the victim of all violence. Emblematic is the fact that his death brought together "Herod and Pontius Pilate, with the Gentiles and the peoples of Israel" (Acts 4:27); the onetime enemies became friends, as always happens in a crisis where a scapegoat is involved.

Christ defeated violence not by opposing it with greater violence, but by undergoing it and exposing all its injustice and uselessness. (If nothing else, Mel Gibson's film, *The Passion of the Christ*, had the merit of reminding us of the extremes of violence inflicted on Jesus.) He inaugurated a new kind of victory, which St. Augustine

---

119. *Things Hidden Since the Foundation of the World* (Stanford, CA: University Press, 1987), this is the title of the work in which Girard describes this new phase of his research.

summarized in three words: *"Victor quia victima"* ("Victor because victim").[120] By raising Jesus from death, the Father has declared once and for all where truth and justice are to be found, and where there is error and falsehood. The process that leads to the birth of religion is reversed; in Christ, it is God who makes himself a victim, and not the victim who is subsequently elevated to divine dignity. Christ did not come with another's blood, but with his own. He did not lay his own sins on others' backs—men or animals; he laid the sins of others on his own back: "He himself bore our sins in his body on the tree" (1 Pt 2:24). A whole theology is contained in the title, "Lamb of God," with which the liturgy twice salutes Christ during the Mass.

4. Can We Still Speak of Sacrifice?

Theologians (among them Hans Urs von Balthasar) welcomed Girard's analysis with great interest, seeing in it the basis for an understanding of the mystery of redemption that responds to modern sensitivities. However, they also felt the need to complete his analysis from a strictly theological point of view. The most important "correction" refers to the type of solution that Christ gives to the problem of violence and of evil in general. Salvation does not come only from having revealed the unconscious mechanism that generates violence; in other words, it is not only of a cognitive and psychological nature, but also mystical. There is "something more" in Christ's death, which the Bible and theology express with the terms "expiation" and "vicarious substitution." Evil, which

---

120. Augustine, *Confessions*, X, 43.

violence both symbolizes and encapsulates, is not only denounced, but also "destroyed."[121]

Can one still continue to speak of sacrifice in reference to the death of Christ and consequently the Mass? For a long time Girard refuted this concept, considering it too marked by the idea of violence, but he eventually admitted the possibility on condition of seeing Christ's death as an entirely new kind of sacrifice, and of seeing in this change of meaning "the central event in the religious history of humanity."

The story of the two mothers and of Solomon's judgment (cf. 1 Kings 3:16–28) convinced him of the possibility of a different type of sacrifice, which derives its meaning from love. In that case, both mothers are prepared to give up the child, but for one of them, the false mother, the sacrifice is only made out of revenge; for the true mother, it is only out of love.

The novelty of Christ's sacrifice is highlighted from different points of view in the Letter to the Hebrews: Christ had no need to offer victims first of all for his own sins, like every priest (7:27); he had no need to repeat the sacrifice several times, but "once for all at the end of the age to put away sin by the sacrifice of himself" (9:26). The novelty of Christ's sacrifice is apparent also from the fact that in the usual sacrifices those who slew the victim were called sacrificers, or priests; in his case they are simply executioners.[122]

---

121. Cf. H. U. von Balthasar, *Theodramatik: Dritte Band, Die Handlung* (Einsiedeln: Johannes Verlag, 1980), p. 309ff.; cf. Kirvan, pp. 106–110.

122. On the new understanding and acceptance of the idea of "sacrifice" by Girard, see his essay "Théorie mimetique et théologie," in R. Girard, *Celui par qui le scandale arrive* (Paris: Arléa, 2001), pp. 63–82.

Some might wish to put aside all idea of expiation in reference to Christ's death and speak only of love. "Christ," it is said, "did not die in order to expiate, but to deposit inside the hard kernel of death the seed of his love. If he died a violent death, the victim of hatred, it was not in order to pay in men's stead their unpayable debt (the debt of ten thousand talents was condoned by the king!), but simply so that suffering and death would henceforth be inhabited by love, and human beings, on entering them, would find the love of Christ awaiting them even there." But we are not forced to choose necessarily between expiation and love. Both can coexist: sin is cancelled out, washed away, destroyed, in a word, "expiated," by its contrary, which is love, not simply by the suffering and death of Christ.

We know what caused the notion of sacrifice to be applied so forcefully to the death of Christ, without due distinctions being made, just as we are familiar with the disturbing question (still awaiting a satisfactory answer): "To whom was the price of the ransom paid?" All this has given rise to the idea of the "implacable" Father, and, consequently, the instinctive rejection by many of a Father-God to the point of proclaiming, with a sigh of relief, "the death of God."

Looking at it more deeply, we see that the Father does not appear so much as the one who receives the ransom as the one who pays it. In fact, he pays the highest price of all, because he has given his only Son. To say that the Father "did not spare his own Son" (Rom 8:32), is the same as saying that "he has not spared himself."

5. Out of Love or Obedience?

How is all this reconciled with the New Testament affirmation (see Rom 5:19 and Phil 2:8!) that Christ died "out of obedience" to the Father? We must first of all recall what Jesus himself declares in St. John's Gospel: "For this reason the Father loves me, because I lay down my life, that I may take it up again. No one takes it from me, but I lay it down of my own accord. I have power to lay it down, and I have power to take it up again; this charge I have received from my Father" (Jn 10:17–18).

Here he speaks of a "power" to offer his life and of a "command" to do so, of freedom and obedience; but the key to the mystery lies precisely in this paradox. How and when did the Father give the Son the "command" to offer his life freely? According to St. Thomas, the Father delivered the Son to death "inasmuch as he inspired him with the will to suffer for us, infusing love into him."[123] The "command" that the Son received from the Father is, therefore, first of all, the command to love us. Transmitting to the Son his nature, which is love, the Father transmitted to him, along with it, his "passionate love" for humanity, and this passionate love led Jesus to the cross!

Yes, Jesus died for love of us, but that was precisely his obedience to the Father! The most perfect obedience does not lie in perfectly carrying out the order received, but in making one's own the will of the person who gives it. Christ's obedience was like this. The Second Eucharistic Prayer expresses this vision of Christ's death in a formula that goes back to the very beginnings of the Christian liturgy: "Before he was given up to death, a death he freely accepted...."[124]

---

123. Aquinas, *S.Th.*, III, q. 47, a. 3.

124. The formula goes back to the *Traditio Apostolica* of Hippolytus, 4: B. Botte, *La tradition Apostolique de St. Hippolyte*, Münster in W., 1963, p. 14: *"Qui cum traderetur voluntariae passioni..."*

St. Bernard's insights about this were ahead of his time. Anticipating the objections of people today, Abelard had written: "Did the death of his innocent Son so please God the Father as to make him reconciled with us through it?" The saint responded: "It was not Christ's death that pleased the Father, but his will to die spontaneously for us."[125] Another of Abelard's objections was: "Who would not think it cruel and unjust for someone to request the blood of an innocent man in recompense, or at any rate that he should be pleased that an innocent man be killed? Could God have considered his Son's death so pleasing as to reconcile the whole world to himself through him?" St. Bernard replies with the concise statement: "God the Father did not request his Son's blood; he only accepted it once it was offered; he had no thirst for that blood, but for our salvation, which resided in that blood."[126]

It is true that in Isaiah it is said of the Servant: "The Lord *was pleased* to crush him with suffering" (53:10). But, we ask ourselves, was he really "pleased"? What, exactly, pleased him? He was not pleased by the means, but by the end! Not by the Servant's suffering, but by the salvation of many, as St. Bernard noted. What truly pleased God, and what he did with great joy, is what he proclaims in the first person in the sequel to the passage: "Therefore I will divide him a portion with the great, and he shall

---

125. St. Bernard of Clairvaux, *Letter 90, De errore Abelardi*, 8, 21–22 (PL 182, 1070): *"Non mors, sed voluntas placuit sponte morientis."*

126. Ibid.: *"Non requisivit Deus Pater sanguinem Filii, sed tamen acceptavit oblatum."* St. Bernard in turn depends on St. Anselm of Canterbury, *Meditatio redemptionis humanae*, ed. F.S. Schmitt, *Opera omnia*, III (Stuttgart, 1968), p. 88: "The Father did not command the Man Christ to die, but it was he who did so spontaneously, knowing that this would please the Father and would be beneficial to mankind."

divide the spoil with the strong; because he poured out his soul to death" (53:12).

"Scripture grows with those who read it *(crescit cum legentibus),*" wrote St. Gregory the Great,[127] and this also occurred with the passages about Christ's sacrifice and the redemption. The events and experiences of the twentieth century, never before lived by humanity on such a scale, have posed new questions to Scripture, and Scripture's replies, as always, have met the measure of the questions.

The analysis of violence and the sacred also casts new light on the abolition of the death penalty. Something of the scapegoat mechanism is at work in every execution, even in those sanctioned by law. "One has died for all" (2 Cor 5:14): the believer now has an added Eucharistic reason to be opposed to the death penalty. How can some Christians, in certain countries, approve and rejoice on hearing the news that a criminal has been condemned to death when we read in the Bible: "Have I any pleasure in the death of the wicked, says the Lord God, and not rather that he should turn from his way and live?" (Ez 18:23).

The modern debate on violence and the sacred thus helps us to take in a new dimension of the Eucharist. Thanks to it, God's absolute "no" to violence, delivered on the cross, is kept alive through the centuries. The Eucharist is the sacrament of nonviolence! At the same time, it appears to us, positively, as God's "yes" to innocent victims, the place where every day the blood that is spilt on earth is united to that of Christ, which cries out to God "with a voice more eloquent than that of Abel" (Heb

---

127. Gregory the Great, *Commentary on Job*, XX, 1 (CC 143 A, p. 1,003).

12:24). From this one understands also what would be removed from the Mass (and the world!) if this dramatic character, expressed from time immemorial in the word sacrifice, is taken away from it.

6. The Blood of Christ Cleanses Us from All Sin

Finally, let us look at the invocation that the *Adoro Te Devote* places on our lips after the words: "a single drop, for sinners spilt, is ransom for a world's entire guilt." The invocation is: "O loving Pelican! O Jesus, Lord! Unclean I am, but cleanse me in Thy blood."

The invocation does not seem to be very consistent with the symbol. According to the legend, the pelican does not wound its breast to wash its young, but to feed them and bring them back to life. We must keep in mind that, as in the case of the good thief or the apostle Thomas, the symbol "launches" the reflection, it does not imprison it. We see this in the thoughts that our stanza inspired in Claudel in his magnificent *Hymn to the Most Holy Sacrament:*

> Loving Pelican that before our eyes suffer your
>   crucifixion,
> served by weeping angels holding ciborium and paten,
> open to us the door of your side as to the centurion,
> so that we will have access to you and be able to
>   unite
> our nature to your hypostasis.[128]

The famous prayer, *Anima Christi*, which is also found in St. Pius V's Missal among the prayers of thanks-

---

128. P. Claudel, *Hymne du Saint Sacrement*, in *Oeuvre poétique*, p. 400.

giving at Mass, sees in the Eucharistic blood the source of spiritual inebriation: "Soul of Christ, sanctify me. Body of Christ, save me. Blood of Christ, inebriate me" ("Anima Christi, santifica me. Corpus Christi, salva me. Sanguis Christi, inebria me").

However, the author was not wrong to emphasize the purification from sins through the blood. It is an exquisitely biblical theme. The most direct source is Revelation 1:5 which, in the Vulgate text familiar to the author, said: "He has loved us and has *washed* us from our sins with his blood." The connection between the blood and the remission of sins is already affirmed in the words of the institution: "This is the cup of my blood...shed for you and for all so that sins may be forgiven." The apostolic catechesis never tires of repeating the fact: "The blood of Jesus cleanses us from all sin" (1 Jn 1:7); "The blood of Christ purifies our conscience from dead works" (Heb 9:14). In the Mass it is possible for us to undergo each time a sort of spiritual dialysis: the debris of sin that accumulates in our conscience is dispelled by contact with the blood of Christ that comes into us under the sign of wine.

7. To Become a Victim, Not to Victimize!

In the light of these reflections, however, we cannot fail to refer to one particular sin, which we must decide to be cleansed from by the power that comes from the Eucharistic blood of Christ: the sin that is the basis of the scapegoat mechanism and violence that Jesus came to denounce and break. History has taught us a bitter lesson. Christ died to destroy the mechanism that leads to the scapegoat, but in some cases Christians have done precisely what Christ came to abolish. The treatment of Jews is a case in point.

At the personal level, the sin we must be aware of is the tendency to systematically excuse ourselves and accuse others, to make victims, rather than making ourselves a victim. He, the Innocent One, accepted being considered guilty; we, the guilty, seek at all costs to be regarded as innocent.

There is a violence that is not only of hands and weapons, but also of thoughts. A desert Father offers clear and strong words in this respect: "If we fail to make headway on our journey, to make ourselves useful in some way, it is because we spend our time brooding over our thoughts against one another and tormenting ourselves. Everyone justifies himself, obeys nothing, and then expects others to give an account of how they observe the commandments."[129] How much good would accrue to ecclesial communion itself if we all made an effort to follow the way of the Lamb, and stopped blaming those who think differently from us for all the ills of the Church or of the community we live in.

As always, we do not want the last thought to be one of guilt, but one of grace. The Eucharist does more than remind us of Christ's example; it also gives us the grace to follow him. His victory was also for us, and, in faith, we can appropriate to ourselves his victory over violence and try to translate it into concrete attitudes in life.

We find in a hymn by Charles Wesley, who founded the Methodist Church with his brother, John, the same sentiments of unworthiness and confidence in the purifying power of Christ's blood that inspire the present stan-

---

129. Dorotheus of Gaza, *Instructions*, 7 (SCh 92, p. 300).

za of the *Adoro Te Devote*. We conclude the present meditation with the words of the hymn, happy to share our love of the Eucharist with Christians of other denominations in the hope of being able to share with them, one day, the Eucharist itself:

I am not worthy, Lord,
so foul, so self-abhorr'd,
Thee, my God, to entertain
In this polluted heart:
I am a frail sinful man,
all my nature cries, Depart!

Yet come, thou heavenly Guest,
and purify my breast;
Come, thou great and glorious King,
while before Thy cross I bow,
with Thyself salvation bring,
Cleanse the house by entering now.[130]

---

130. C. Wesley, hymn: *Savior, and can it be,* in John and Charles Wesley, *Selected Writings and Hymns* (New York: Paulist Press, 1981), p. 257ff.

VII.

Jesus! Whom Veil'd I See...

The Eucharist and the Return of Creatures to God

1. A Profound and Personal Devotion

As we have seen, the *Adoro Te Devote* reflects an eminently individual and personal devotion. All the verbs are in the first person singular: *adoro, credo, peto, intueor, oro, aspicio;* all the pronouns and possessive adjectives refer to an "I" or a "Thou": *me, te, tibi, cor meum, Deum meum, meae menti.* The one praying is alone before Christ; there is no reference to a celebrating community; there is no liturgical dimension.

This is explained, in part, by the Eucharistic practice of the time, which was totally concentrated on the real presence and neglected the communal dimension of the sacrament. Such was the fear that the importance given to the presence of the *ecclesial body* of Christ in the Eucharist might compromise the unique character of the presence of his *real body,* that exclamations like those St. Augustine addressed to the people were no longer heard: "You are the body of Christ and his members; it is your mystery therefore that is celebrated on the altar!"[131]

I mention this not to criticize the practice of the past, but, if anything, to appreciate what the Spirit is giving us to live in the Church today, to assess the progress and return to a theology and a Eucharistic practice that is closer to that of the Fathers and more in keeping with the communal nature of the sacrament.

As is always the case, however, a one-sided emphasis in one context can become a useful corrective in another. Today, when the social and communal dimension of the Church and the Eucharist ("the Eucharist makes the Church!") is so keenly felt, the call of the *Adoro Te Devote* to a profound, personal devotion is providential.

> The unity of Christ's members will not be achieved either by the human fact of coming together for the celebration of the mysteries, or the collective enthusiasm provoked by an appropriate pedagogy. Such unity is impossible without the remission of sins, first fruit of the blood shed by the Lord. The Memorial of the Passion, offered to the heavenly Father, and conversion of heart are the indispensable inner dispositions, without which there will only be a caricature of the much desired community.[132]

The community may become an alibi or a way of avoiding that most singular question addressed by Christ to Martha: "Do you believe?" and the one he puts to Peter and every disciple after him: "Do you love me?" A crowd of people with dulled faith does not constitute a

---

131. St. Augustine, *Sermo*, 272 (PL 38, 1247).
132. H. de Lubac, *Corpus mysticum*, p. 293ff.

community of "believers," just as thousands of drops of cold water do not make a tub of hot water.

On this question the world's cultures oscillate from one extreme to the other. At one point they exalt the universal (the community aspect), at another, the particular (that of the individual). At times they believe that history is made by great individual personalities, at others, by the masses. Faith provides a synthesis of the two extremes and values both the individual and the comunity. For Christ, the "flock" is important (united under one shepherd); equally important is the individual "sheep," which he knows by name (cf. Jn 10:3), and for which he is ready to leave the rest of the flock unguarded for a while (cf. Lk 15:4ff.). The Fathers summarized all this in the formula *"Ecclesia vel anima"* ("the Church and the soul").

Far from considering the *Adoro Te Devote* outdated and useless today, now is the time for us to rediscover its beauty and to sing it more vigorously than ever. In this spirit, we now meditate on the last stanza of the hymn, where the profound, personal dimension is once again clearly visible.

2. Pledge of Future Glory

Different manuscripts state that the *Adoro Te Devote* was "the prayer that St. Thomas Aquinas pronounced on his deathbed at the moment of receiving the Eucharist."[133] If this were a fact, the hymn's last stanza would acquire an altogether particular, autobiographical meaning. It says:

---

133. Cf. G. M. Dreves, *Lateinische Hymnendichter des Mittelalters*, II, (AHMA, 50, Lipsia 1907), p. 590ff.

Jesu quem velátum nunc aspício,
oro fiat illud quod tam sítio:
ut, te reveláta cernens fácie,
visu sim beátus tuae glóriae. Amen.[134]

Jesus! Whom for the present veil'd I see,
what I so thirst for, O vouchsafe to me:
that I may see Thy countenance unfolding,
and may be blest Thy glory in beholding. Amen.

However, we have a detailed account of the saint's last hours from his disciple and eyewitness, William of Tocco, who makes no reference to our hymn with the exception of the addition found on the margin of a late manuscript, whose authenticity is anything but certain.[135] However, all this is secondary as we are more interested in the content of the hymn than in the author.

The last stanza of the *Adoro Te Devote* reflects the eschatological dimension that accompanied the Eucharist from the beginning. According to St. Luke, while Jesus was seated at the table, he said: "I have earnestly desired to eat this Passover with you before I suffer; for I tell you I shall not eat it until it is fulfilled in the kingdom of God" (Lk 22:15ff.). Therefore, what Jesus did immediately afterward—the institution of the Eucharist—was in anticipation of the eternal banquet of the Kingdom. From the beginning, believers celebrated the Supper "until he comes" (1 Cor 11:26). Hence the cry that resounded in Christian assemblies: *Marana Tha* (Come, Lord), which

---

134. The critical text reconstructed by Wilmart, instead of *oro fiat illud,* has *quando fiet illud,* which turns this line into a question: "When will my great longing be fulfilled...?"

135. See n. 2 of chap. 1.

continues to resound in different forms today in the acclamation after the consecration.

In the Book of Revelation the Church's Eucharistic worship is seen as a preparation for the eternal liturgy of the elect in the heavenly Jerusalem. The priest's exclamation at the moment of Communion: "Happy are those who are called to his supper," is an adaptation (perhaps not even necessary) of Revelation 19:9: "Blessed are those who are invited to the marriage supper of the Lamb."[136]

It is the very manner of Jesus' presence in the sacrament that arouses a heartfelt expectation and desire for something more. The *Adoro Te Devote* begins by referring to Christ's "hidden" presence and ends by mentioning his "veiled" presence. However, it is precisely his being hidden and veiled that arouses the desire for the unveiling, for the "unveiled vision" *(revelata facie)*. For the one who loves, a hidden and partial presence is not enough. St. John of the Cross speaks of the Eucharist in these words, undoubtedly prompted by experience:

> When I try to find relief
> Beholding You in the Sacrament,
> I find this greater sorrow:
> I cannot enjoy You wholly.
> All things are affliction
> Since I do not see You as I desire,
> And I die because I do not die.[137]

---

136. Cf. S. Hahn, *The Lamb's Supper: The Mass as Heaven on Earth* (New York: Doubleday, 1999).

137. *Stanzas of the soul that suffers with longing to see God.* From *The Collected Works of St. John of the Cross,* translated by Kieran Kavanaugh and Otilio Rodriguez. Copyright © 1964, 1979, 1991 by Washington Province of Discalced Carmelites ICS Publications, 2131 Lincoln Road, N.E. Washington, DC 20002-1199 U.S.A. www.icspublications.org

Perhaps it was precisely in reference to the present stanza of the *Adoro Te Devote* that Bossuet wrote: "Therefore, I have all. What is there left for me to desire if not to see what I possess, to tear the veil and contemplate clearly, by manifest vision, that which I know well I have, but which I still cannot see?"[138]

The Eucharist not only arouses the desire for future glory, but is essentially its pledge: *et futurae gloriae nobis pignus datur* (Antiphon, *O sacrum convivium*). The Holy Spirit is given to us in this world as first fruits and *deposit,* the Eucharist as first fruits and *pledge.* St. Augustine explains this difference: the pledge is not the beginning of the payment, but something that is given in anticipation of it; once the latter is effected, the pledge is returned. Not so the deposit, which is not returned at the moment of payment, but completed, since it is already part of the payment.[139] In this world, the Holy Spirit is like a deposit because when entering eternal life its enjoyment will not be replaced but will reach its fullness. The Eucharist is a pledge because it will cease when signs and sacraments end and are replaced by the vision of glory.

A liturgical prayer states that the Eucharist is "what reveals to us, pilgrims on earth, the Christian meaning of life."[140] Like the manna, it is nourishment for those who are on the way to the Promised Land. It is a constant reminder to the Christian that he is a "pilgrim and stranger" in this world; that his life is an exodus.

---

138. J.-B. Bossuet, *Méditations sur l'Evangile, La Cène,* 49 journée (*Oeuvres complètes,* II, Paris, 1845, p. 554ff.).

139. Augustine, *Sermo,* 23, 9 (CC 41, p. 314).

140. Opening prayer, Monday of the third week of Advent.

In Christian language, the word "viaticum" has eventually come to signify the last Eucharist, the one received at the point of death; but its meaning is far greater. In the *Lauda Sion* sequence, the Eucharistic bread is said to be "food of wayfarers" *(cibus viatorum)* because it sustains us throughout this life's journey and not only in our passing to eternal life. This is the meaning of the episode of Elijah recalled in the Office of *Corpus Christi* as a figure of the Eucharist. Elijah, exhausted by the long journey and worn out by persecution, lies down to die; an angel shows him a cake baked on hot stones and says to him, "Get up and eat!" And again, "Get up and eat, or else the journey will be too much for you." Elijah "arose, and ate and drank, and in the strength of that food traveled forty days and forty nights to Horeb, the mountain of God" (1 Kings 19:1-8).

3. The Eucharist, Canticle of Creatures

Since the New Testament, Christian eschatology has developed two points of view: that of the "consequent" eschatology of the synoptics and of St. Paul, which places fulfillment in the future, at the second coming of Christ, while strongly stressing the dimension of expectation and hope, and that of the "realized" eschatology of St. John, which places the essential fulfillment in the past, in the coming of Christ in the Incarnation, and sees the experience of eternal life as already begun in faith and in the sacraments.

The Eucharist reflects these perspectives. It reflects the "consequent" eschatology inasmuch as it makes us live "in the expectation of his coming"; it impels us to constantly look forward and to perceive ourselves as "wayfarers" in this world—people journeying toward the homeland. It reflects the "realized" eschatology inasmuch as it allows us to taste, here and now, the first fruits of eternal life; it is an open window through which the future world erupts into the present, eternity enters into time, and creatures begin their "return to God."

Let us now consider the Eucharist under this last aspect. In it is fulfilled sacramentally that act which, according to the Apostle, will conclude history: "When all things are subjected to him, then the Son himself will also be subjected to him who put all things under him, that God may be everything to everyone" (1 Cor 15:28). It could be said that we can hasten or retard the attainment of the final purpose of history. Christ, in fact, is not "wholly" subjected while there is one member of his body that is not subjected to him. "So long as I am not subjected to the Father neither can it be said that Christ is subjected to him. He does not want to receive his full glory without you; namely, without his people, who are his body and his members."[141]

The Eucharist comes to meet us in this endeavor. In it we subject ourselves to Christ who offers us with himself to the Father, as the final doxology of the Canon proclaims: "Through him, with him, in him, in the unity of the Holy Spirit, all glory and honor is yours, Almighty Father, for ever and ever. Amen."

The whole of human activity and creation itself returns to God thanks to the Eucharist. In the bread and wine, "fruits of the earth and work of human hands," is the material itself—sun, earth, water—presented to God on the altar and achieves its ultimate purpose: to proclaim the Creator's glory. Through them human work also is

---

141. Origen, *Homilies on Leviticus*, 7, 2 (GCS 6, 1920, p. 376).

present on the altar. And this is true not only of agricultural work. In the process that leads from the seed to the bread and from the grapevine to the wine in the chalice, industry intervenes, with its machines, trade, transport, and a myriad other human activities.

In an essay on "The Eucharist and Everyday Life," Karl Rahner wonders how one overcomes the apparent unbridgeable gap between the Eucharist and daily life. In the Eucharist everything is a "holy celebration of God's closeness, the summit of our salvific history and reconciliation of the encounter with the eternal and incarnate Word of God." In daily life, one lives with dreariness, ambiguity, and toil. How then can one be in the world without becoming worldly? "If, when receiving Communion, we also accept everyday life and train ourselves to accept it, then it becomes the continuation of communion in daily reality."[142]

Beyond the daily life of the believer, the Eucharist extends its action to the whole cosmos. As Teilhard de Chardin wrote: "When he (Christ) says through the priest 'This is my body,' his words go well beyond the piece of bread over which they are pronounced: they effect the birth of the whole Mystical Body. Beyond the transubstantiated Host, the priestly action extends to the cosmos itself."[143] Every Eucharist is a "Mass on the world."[144] This vision inspired a prayer of Teilhard de Chardin that we can make our own each time we participate in the Mass and even when we cannot participate:

---

142. K. Rahner, *Eucharistie und altägliches Leben, in Schriften zur Theologie, VII,* (Einsiedeln: Benzinger, 1966), p. 204ff.

143. T. de Chardin, *Comment je crois* (1923), in *Oeuvres,* 10 (Paris: Seuil, 1969), p. 90.

144. T. de Chardin, *La Messe sur le monde* (1923), in *Hymne de l'univers, Oeuvres,* 9 (Paris: Seuil, 1961), p. 17ff.

On the altar of the whole earth I offer you, Lord, the work and the toil of the world.... All that will grow in the world in the course of this day, all that will decline in it, and all that will die in it.... Receive, Lord, this total Host that Creation presents to you, drawn and moved by you, at the dawn of a new day.[145]

Freed from a few ambiguous elements,[146] the doctrine of this extraordinary modern troubadour of the Eucharist could help to give a new power of inspiration to the Sacrament of the Altar by breathing a Eucharistic soul into such current concerns as ecology and the phenomenon of globalization. Such a concept of the Eucharist is actually not entirely new in Christianity. Before Teilhard de Chardin, St. Irenaeus said that the Eucharist, celebrated with bread and wine, which are elements of this world, points to the goodness of creation and somehow sanctifies it.[147] John Paul II himself reflects this same vision when he writes, in an autobiographical vein, in *Ecclesia de Eucharistia:*

I have been able to celebrate Holy Mass in chapels built along mountain paths, on lakeshores and seacoasts; I have celebrated it on altars built in stadiums and in city squares.... This varied scenario of celebrations of the Eucharist has given me a powerful experience of its universal and, so to speak, cosmic character. Yes, cosmic! Because even when it is celebrated on the humble altar of a country church, the Eucharist is always in some way celebrated *on the al-*

145. Ibid., pp. 17–19.

146. Sometimes he also calls the action exerted by the Eucharist on the cosmos a "true universal transsubstantiation" *("une véritable transsubstantiation universelle")* (cf. *Le Christique* [1955]), while elsewhere making a distinction between the two.

147. Cf. St. Irenaeus, *Adv. Haer.,* IV, 17, 5; 18, 5.

tar of the world. It unites heaven and earth. It embraces and permeates all creation.[148]

As can be seen, the Eucharist recapitulates and unifies everything. It reconciles matter and spirit, nature and grace, the sacred and the profane. It is the most sacred and, at the same time, the most secular of the sacraments. It is not only the sacrament of believers, but of all. It is truly the "canticle of creatures."

4. The Wine That Gladdens the Heart of Man

By the very fact that the Eucharist reminds us where we are going, what our final glorious destiny is, and gives us some "foretaste" of that future glory, it is the source from which a Christian's hope and joy are daily renewed. Jesus indicated this festive, joyous meaning of the Eucharist by the sign of wine. Why did he wish to hide his blood in the sign of wine? Was it just the affinity of the color? What does wine represent for people? "In life, wine stands for poetry and color.... It is like dancing compared with just walking. It is playing compared with working."[149] It represents not so much what is useful, like bread, but what is delightful. It is made not just for drinking, but also for proposing a toast. In the desert, Jesus multiplied the loaves for the people's need, but at Cana he multiplied the wine for the guests' delight.

Scripture says that "wine gladdens the heart of man and bread sustains his strength" (Ps 104:15). If Jesus had chosen bread and water for the Eucharist, he would have

148. *Ecclesia de Eucharistia,* no. 8.

149. L. Alonso Schökel, *Celebrating the Eucharist. Biblical Meditations* (London: St. Paul Publications, 1988), p. 70.

indicated only the sanctification of suffering ("bread and water" are in fact synonymous with fasting, austerity, and penance). By choosing bread and wine, he wanted to indicate also the sanctification of joy. In the Bible, the new wine is a symbol of the messianic banquet (cf. Is 25:6) and, in Jesus' words, of the eternal banquet in the Kingdom (cf. Mt 26:29).

But how can the same sign represent suffering and sacrifice (as blood) and joy (as wine)? Surely the two are mutually exclusive? No, not if we think of the sacrifice as offered out of love, as Christ's was. The wine, which the Bible often calls "the blood of the grape," recalls the mysterious relationship that exists, in human experience, between love and sacrifice. "One does not live in love without sorrow," says the *Imitation of Christ.* For a young married couple, the arrival of their first child involves many sacrifices, but also brings great joy! The Eucharistic wine represents the joy of sacrifice!

Gaudium et Spes, the Second Vatican Council's Constitution on the Church in the Modern World, begins: "The joys and the hopes, the griefs and the anxieties of the men of this age, especially those who are poor or in any way afflicted, these are the joys and hopes, the griefs and anxieties of the followers of Christ. Indeed, nothing genuinely human fails to raise an echo in their hearts." There is nothing—we can add—that does not find an echo in the Eucharist. In it, all the sorrow and all the joy of humankind is gathered and offered to God at one and the same time.

We find it very natural to turn to God in times of sorrow. In fact, many of us do not turn to God except when some misfortune makes us realize our need of him. But in joys, on the contrary, we prefer to enjoy on our own, hidden, and almost unknown to God. (In case he suddenly realizes we have had our share of happiness, and now we are ready to go back to pain!) When we receive some joy in life we sometimes behave like a dog that has been given a bone by its owner and immediately turns its back on him and goes off to enjoy it at a distance for fear that it will be taken away.

And yet, how wonderful it would be if we also learned how to live the joys of life eucharistically, in other words, with thanksgiving to God. God's presence and gaze do not diminish our honest joys; on the contrary, they enlarge them. With God, little joys become an incentive to aspire to eternal joy when, as our stanza sings, "we will see his countenance unfolding, and be blest his glory in beholding."

5. A Doctrine Born of Life

At the beginning we mentioned the claim that the *Adoro Te Devote* was the prayer that St. Thomas Aquinas addressed to Christ as he was dying. The claim, we noted, remains doubtful, but the account that his biographer, William of Tocco, gives of the holy Doctor's last moments of life is, in itself, an extraordinary testimony of Eucharistic devotion and reveals the source of the doctrine that, directly or indirectly, inspired the most beautiful Eucharistic texts of the Latin Church, including the *Adoro Te Devote*. It is worth reading in full:

> Feeling his strength failing and sensing the nearness of his departure from this world, the holy Doctor, with great devotion, requested the viaticum of the Christian pilgrimage, the Most Holy Body and Blood of Christ. After the abbot and the monks had brought the Eu-

charist to him, he prostrated himself on the ground, weak in body but strong in spirit, and went, with tears, to meet his Lord. Then, in the presence of the sacrament of the Body of Christ, as is the custom with every Christian at the moment of death, he was asked if he believed that in that consecrated host was the true Son of God, born of the womb of the Virgin, suspended from the scaffold of the cross, who died and rose for us on the third day. With a free voice and great devotion mingled with tears, he replied: "I truly believe and hold as certain that he is true God and true man, Son of God the Father and of the Virgin Mother, and I believe with my heart and profess with my lips that which the priest has asked me of this most Holy Sacrament." And after some words of devotion [at this point the addition places the *Adoro Te Devote!*], receiving the sacrament he exclaimed: "I receive you, price of the redemption of my soul, for love of which I have studied, watched, and worked; I have preached and taught you; I have said nothing against you nor am I obstinate in my opinion; if in some part I have spoken poorly of this sacrament, I submit all to the correction of the Holy Roman Church, in whose obedience I pass from this life."[150]

May we also, at the end of life, be able to say the same as St. Thomas Aquinas! These are the sentiments with which I also wished to develop my reflections on the *Adoro Te Devote* and I now humbly submit them to the Church.

We end with the last two stanzas of the *Lauda Sion*, the Eucharistic hymn which, probably more than others, may be attributed to the Angelic Doctor. They transport us

---

150. William de Tocco, *Ystoria*, p. 197ff.

to the same climate of expectation and joyful hope as the
last stanza of the *Adoro Te Devote:*

> *Tu, qui cuncta scis et vales,*
> *qui nos pascis hic mortáles:*
> *tuos ibi commensáles*
> *coherédes et sodáles,*
> *fac sanctórum cívium.*

> Source of all we have or know,
> feed and lead us here below.
> Grant that with your saints above,
> sitting at the feast of love
> we may see you face to face.

Hail, True Body, Truly Born of the Virgin Mary

With Us Until the End of the World

1. The *Ave Verum*

After having gathered some of the treasures of the *Adoro Te Devote*, in this last meditation we reflect on the message that comes from another equally well-known and cherished Eucharistic hymn, the *Ave Verum*. Although different in length and form, the two hymns were born in the same theological and spiritual climate and witness to the same type of Eucharistic devotion.

The oldest manuscripts of the text date back to the end of the thirteenth and the beginning of the fourteenth centuries. The names of several possible authors have been suggested, but as in the case of the *Adoro Te Devote*, his identity remains uncertain.[151] Perhaps this is a good

---

151. Cf. C. Blume and H. M. Bannister, *Thesaurus Himnology Prosarum*, I, 2, Leipzig, 1915 (AHMA, 54), p. 258. The name most often mentioned is that of Pope Innocent IV, given the fact that the hymn was composed in the North of Italy, that the oldest manuscript comes from Genoa, the Pope's native land, was written forty years after his death

thing, because it highlights even more the choral character of the hymn, which belongs to all those who have ever sung it or prayed with it no less than to the author. The hymn is extremely simple. It has five verses (trochaic tetrameters) with rhyme, or assonance, both in the central caesurae and at the end of each verse. The text presents some variations in the manuscripts but, for the reasons just given, we prefer to keep to the traditional text, used in Gregorian chant and admirably set to music by Mozart:

> *Ave verum corpus natum de Maria Virgine.*
> *Vere passum, immolatum in cruce pro homine.*
> *Cuius latus perforatum fluxit aqua et sanguine.*
> *Esto nobis praegustatum mortis in examine.*
> *O Iesu dulcis, O Iesu pie, O Iesu fili Mariae.*

> Hail, true Body, truly born of the Virgin Mary mild.
> Truly offered, wracked and torn, on the cross for
>   all defiled,
> from whose love-pierced, sacred side flowed Thy
>   true blood's saving tide:
> be a foretaste sweet to me in my death's great
>   agony.
> O my loving, Gentle One, Sweetest Jesus, Mary's
>   Son.[152]

The conclusion is a conscious evocation of the last words of the Salve Regina: *"O clemens, O pia, O dulcis virgo Maria"* ("O clement, O loving, O sweet Virgin Mary").

(1254), and that the same Pope conferred special indulgences on the text. But what we know of the character of that Pontiff is hard to reconcile with the hymn's profound piety.

152. Trans. Edward Francis Garesche, S.J.

2. From the "Mystical" Body to the "True" Body

The first verse provides the key to understanding all the rest. There is a whole history behind the expression "true body" *(verum corpus)*, masterfully reconstructed by Henri de Lubac.[153] From the Fathers until roughly the beginning of the second millennium, the body of Christ in the Eucharist was defined as his "mystical" body, or his spiritual, sacramental body, to distinguish it from the material and historical body, born of Mary, which suffered under Pontius Pilate and died on the cross. By defining the Eucharistic body of Christ as *mystical (or spiritual, in sacrament, in figure)* the authors were not denying but rather affirming the reality and objectivity of his presence.

The "turning point" that led to a change of language began in the ninth century. "Mystical" was no longer understood as synonymous with "true" but, in a certain sense, as its contrary. "True," not "mystical," was now the mark of Eucharistic orthodoxy. The term did not disappear from use but now referred only to the ecclesial body, until it became the current definition of the Church, the "Mystical Body of Christ." The evolution gathered pace in the eleventh century because of the heresy of Berengarius of Tours, who denied the reality of the presence of Christ in the sign of bread, reducing it to a symbolic presence. The total identity between the Eucharistic and the historical body of Christ began to be affirmed to remove every pretext for this heresy.

---

153. Cf. H. de Lubac, *Corpus mysticum: L'Eucharistie et l'Eglise au Moyen age* (Paris: Aubier, 1949).

This is the stage reflected in the *Ave Verum*. Proof of this is the expression "true body" *(verum corpus)*, used here in tacit opposition to "mystical body," as well as the insistence on the identity between the Eucharistic body of Christ and that born of Mary, which suffered on the cross and from whose side flowed blood and water. The author stops at that point; he makes no mention of the resurrection, lest this should lead one to think of a glorified, spiritual body, not sufficiently "real."

Today we must complete the *Ave Verum* on this point. The "true" body of Christ is not only the one that was born, died, and pierced on the cross; it is also the risen body living in the Spirit. If the "true body" of Christ born of Mary is on the altar, it is because it is risen; otherwise it would not be his living body, but only a dead relic. The image that best describes the "state" of Christ in the Eucharist is that of the Lamb of Revelation "standing, as though it had been slain" (Rev 5:6). Immolated, namely, dead, and with the wounds still visible, but at the same time standing, on its feet, risen and alive.

3. The Eucharist, God-with-Us

In our day, theology has returned to a more nuanced view of the identity between the historical body of Christ, born of Mary, and his Eucharistic body. With the ending of the controversy that led to this identity being affirmed with few distinctions, the tendency is to rediscover the sacramental character of Christ's presence, which, though real and substantial, is not material. However, underneath this difference of emphasis, the truth affirmed in the hymn remains intact. It is the Jesus born of Mary at Bethlehem, the very same who "went about doing good and healing all" (Acts 10:38), who died on the cross and rose again on the third day, who is really present in the world today, not in some vague and spiritual way, or, as some say, in the "cause" for which he stood. The Eucharist is the way invented by God so that he can remain forever Emmanuel, God-with-us.

This presence is a guarantee and a protection not only for the Church, but for the entire world. Now we almost feel afraid to use the words "God is with us," because they have sometimes been used in an exclusive sense: God is "with us," meaning not with others, or even "against" those others who are our enemies. But now that Christ has come, there is no longer any exclusiveness, everything has become universal. "God in Christ was reconciling the world to himself, not counting their trespasses against them" (2 Cor 5:19)—reconciling the whole world, not just a part of it, humankind as a whole, not just one people.

"God is on our side," that is, on the side of humankind, our friend and ally against the powers of evil. God alone personifies the kingdom of good against the kingdom of evil. This gave Dietrich Bonhöffer, in prison awaiting the death sentence from Hitler's "evil power," the strength to believe in the final victory of God's good power:

> By kindly powers so wonderfully protected
> we wait with confidence, befall what may.
> We are with God at night and in the morning
> and, just as certainly, on each new day.[154]

As the pope writes in *Novo Millennio Ineunte,* "We do not know what the new millennium has in store for us,

---

154. Trans. John Brownjohn.

but we are certain that it is safe in the hands of Christ, the 'King of kings and Lord of lords' (Rev 19:16)."[155]

The *Ave Verum* is a call to live with joy and thanksgiving the "time of the Church" in which we find ourselves. It assures us that we are not living in "weak" times or in a situation of retreat, like someone who, not having met a loved one in real life has to make do with knowing them through a photograph. We must not say of Christ's days on earth: "Those were the days, those were the days," as if only something that happened once, the first time, were true and interesting and everything else thereafter empty repetition.

This is the lament of the ardent Joan of Arc in Péguy's play. Driven by her burning love for Christ, she envies the woman who washed his feet (his real feet of flesh!), the Veronica who wiped his face (his real, fleshly face!), the Cyrenian who helped him carry the cross (the real cross, made of wood!). "What had those people done for you, then, my God," she exclaims, "to be so highly honored, so favored, so fortunate, so blessed, so graced by that grace?" All that came afterward was a patchwork in comparison, a poor second best.

This moving but exaggerated nostalgia for the first time, the only time, the unrepeatable, historic, once-and-for-all time, is countered by the response of the character in the play who represents the Catholic Church. He states that there is nothing to regret because

> He is here among us as on the day of his death....
> His body, his same body, hangs on the same cross...
> It is the same story...that happened at that time and in
>   that country

---

155. *Novo Millennio Ineunte*, no. 35.

and it happens every day....
In all the parishes in all of Christendom.[156]

This is the consequence of the great principle formulated by St. Leo the Great: "All that was visible in our Lord Jesus Christ has passed into the sacraments of the Church."[157] In the Eucharist we can still wash his feet like Magdalene, welcome him like Martha and Mary, help him carry his cross like the Cyrenian.... True, we can also serve him in the person of the poor, but there we minister to him through an "intermediary," while here we serve him "in person."

4. Pledge of Future Glory

After the initial greeting, heavy with theological implications, the hymn continues with an invocation: *Esto nobis praegustatum mortis in examine* (be a foretaste in my death's great agony). Long ago, the martyr, Ignatius of Antioch called the Eucharist "the medicine of immortality."[158] "Nourished with the body and blood of Christ," says St. Irenaeus, "buried in the earth and dissolved our bodies will rise in due time because the Word of God shall give them resurrection for the glory of God"; "We will rise," exclaims St. Cyril of Alexandria, "because Christ is in us through his very flesh."[159] In the Eucharist we have "the pledge of future glory" *("futurae gloriae nobis pignus datur")*.

---

156. C. Péguy, *Joan of Arc's Mystery of Charity,* in *Oeuvres Poétiques Completes* (Paris: Pléiade, 1975), pp. 400–413.

157. St. Leo the Great, *Discourse on the Ascension, 2* (PL 54, 398).

158. St. Ignatius of Antioch, *Letter to the Ephesians,* 20, 2.

159. St. Irenaeus, *Adv. Haer.,* V, 2, 3; St. Cyril of Alexandria, *On the Gospel of John,* IV, 2 (PG 73, 581).

Some religious surveys have revealed a strange fact: there are, even among believers, some who believe in God, but not in a life after death. Yet how could one think such a thing? The Letter to the Hebrews says that Christ died to obtain "an eternal redemption" for us (9:12). The redemption, then, is not just for a time. "Why is it so hard to believe that men will really live with God one day," St. Augustine asked the people, "when we see that an even more incredible fact has already happened, namely that God died for men?"[160]

Some object that no one has ever come back from the afterlife to assure us that it really exists and is not merely an illusion. That is not true! There is someone who comes back from beyond death every day to give us that certainty and to renew his promises, if we but know how to listen to him. We are on our way to meet the one who comes to meet us every day in the Eucharist to give us a foretaste *(praegustatum!)* of the eternal banquet of the Kingdom.

This hope is something we need to cry out to the world to help ourselves and others overcome the horror of death and the mood of gloomy pessimism that hovers over our society. So many reasons are put forward for the desperate state of the world: "an anthill crumbling away," "a planet in its death throes...." Scientists sketch in ever-greater detail the possible scenario for the dissolution of the cosmos. The earth and other planets will grow cold, the sun and other stars will cool down, everything will grow cold.... Light will fade, and black holes will increase in the universe, until eventually expansion ceases, and contraction begins, and all matter and all energy collapses into a compact mass of infinite density. This will be the

160. Augustine, *Sermo*, 218C, 1 (SCh 116, 200).

"big crunch," the massive implosion, and all will return to the silent void that preceded the *"big bang"* of fifteen billion years ago....

This is all hypothetical; no one knows whether things will really go that way or in some other way, but faith gives us the assurance that, whatever may happen, it will not be the total and final end. God did not reconcile the world to himself only to abandon it to nothingness. He did not promise to remain with us until the end of the world only to retreat into his heaven, alone, when that end comes. "I have loved you with an everlasting love," God says in the Bible (Jer 31:3), and God's promises of "everlasting love" are not like human promises.

5. O Sweet Jesus, O Good Jesus!

The *Ave Verum* closes with a cry addressed to Christ: *"O Iesu dulcis, O Iesu pie, O Iesu fili Mariae."* These words evoke for us a tender, wholly evangelical image of Christ: the "loving, gentle" Jesus, merciful and compassionate, who does not break the bruised reed or quench the smoldering wick. The Jesus who once said: "Learn from me; for I am gentle and lowly in heart" (Mt 11:29).

But Christ's meekness is no justification for the violence that is done today to his person. In fact, it makes it all the more strange and odious. In the stanza on the "loving Pelican," we saw how Christ, by his sacrifice, put an end to the perverse mechanism of the scapegoat by undergoing its consequences himself. Sad to say, Christ is once again subjected to that same fate. All the resentment felt by a certain type of secular thinking against recent manifestations of a link between violence and the sacred is unleashed against him. As usual, when a scapegoat is sought, all the fury of the attack is directed at the one who seems the weakest. "Weakest," here is used in the sense that he can be mocked and derided with impunity, without running any risk of retaliation; Christians, after all, long ago renounced any right to use force in defense of their beliefs.

It is not just about the pressure to remove the crucifix from public places and the crib from Christmas folklore. In an unending stream of novels, films, and plays, writers manipulate the figure of Christ under the cover of imaginary and non-existent new documents and discoveries. It is becoming a fashion, a literary genre.

There has always been a tendency to clothe Christ in the garb of one's own time or one's own ideology. But at least in the past this was done for some noble cause, however debatable it may have been. Jesus the idealist, Jesus the socialist, Jesus the revolutionary... Our own age, obsessed as it is with sex, seems unable to portray Jesus in any other way than as a gay man before his time, or as one who taught that salvation comes from union with the feminine principle, for example by marrying Mary Magdalene.

This is trading on the vast resonance of the name of Christ and on all that he means to a large part of humanity, in order to achieve wide publicity at very little cost, or to shock people with advertisements that exploit Gospel symbols and images, such as the Last Supper. This is literary parasitism! Yet if in some extreme cases believers react and phone or write in to protest, some people decry this as intolerance and censorship. These days, at least in the West, intolerance has changed sides: where we used to have *religious* intolerance, we now have intolerance *of religion!*

The very image of the "loving and gentle" Jesus in the *Ave Verum* forbids us from stopping short at the denunciation of abuses. Jesus went beyond nonviolence itself: he preached mercy and love of enemies. Even if Christians were to become a minority regarded with hostility, as is happening to some extent in some countries, the Eucharist does not allow us to shut ourselves in, to indulge in persecution complexes, and to erect walls or bastions between ourselves and the rest of the world. This is the school where we learn "the spirit of Christ," the "style" of his mission.

"I dream of a Church which is an ever-open Holy Door, which embraces all people, is full of compassion, and understands the sorrows and sufferings of humanity, a Church that protects, consoles, and guides every nation toward the Father who loves us." These words were written by the late Cardinal F. X. Van Thuan, imprisoned in inhuman conditions by the Communist regime in Vietnam for thirteen years, nine of which were spent in solitary confinement. What gave him the strength to write those words was the Eucharist, which for years he celebrated in secret, with three drops of wine and one of water in the palm of one hand and a fragment of bread in the other. With the Eucharist, he said, the whole world was present in his cell. In him, and in so many other martyrs of our times, the Eucharist has shown the underlying true reality of what we call, in terms now devalued by familiarity, the "real presence."

6. Jesus, Son of Mary

The last invocation of the *Ave Verum* recalls the person of the Mother: *"O Iesu fili Mariae."* The Virgin is remembered twice in the short hymn: at the beginning and at the end. The insistence on the bond between Mary and the Eucharist is not just a response to a devotional need, but to a theological truth as well. At the time of the Fathers, Christ's birth of Mary was the principal argument against the Docetists, who denied the reality of Christ's body: "Why do we say that Christ is truly man," the Fathers wrote, "if not because he was born of Mary who is a human creature?"[161] Logically, then, that same birth now bears witness to the truth and reality of the body of Christ present in the Eucharist.

In this statement one also sees how Mary exists exclusively "in relation" to Christ. She is the one who has anchored God to earth and to humanity; the one who, in her divine and most human maternity, has forever made God Emmanuel, the God-with-us, in fact, our brother. St. Irenaeus was right to say that whoever does not understand the Incarnation cannot understand the Eucharist either.[162]

It is impossible to love the Eucharist without loving and being grateful to her who gave Christ the human flesh that he, in turn, gives us in the sacrament. The Eucharist would not exist without Mary. The bond between the two was already clear to Christians from the very first hour. In the typical allusive language of the age of persecutions, Abercius' famous inscription at the end of the second century speaks of "a fish that emerged from the water, very large and very pure, caught by an immaculate virgin,"

---

161. Tertullian, *De Carne Christi*, 5, 6 (CC 2, p. 881).
162. St. Irenaeus, *Against the Heresies*, V, 2, 3 (SCh 153, pp. 34ff.).

which the Church gives to friends to eat.[163] The fish, as we know from so many ancient representations, was the symbol of Christ and the Eucharist, and the virgin is Mary.

We end our reflections with a poem of St. John of the Cross that takes us back to the very source of the Eucharist, the Trinity. With an image familiar to the Fathers of the Church he presents the Father as the well, the Son as the river, and the Holy Spirit as the stream flowing from both, and he concludes that we receive this abundance of "water" in the Blessed Sacrament, even if in an obscure way, as we walk still in faith and not in vision:

> *Aquesta eterna fonte está escondida*
> *En este vivo pan por darnos vida,*
> > *Aunque es de noche.*

> *Aquí se está, llamando a las criaturas,*
> *Y de esta agua se hartan, aunque a oscuras,*
> > *Porque es de noche.*

> *Aquesta viva fuente, que deseo,*
> *En este pan de vida yo la veo,*
> > *Aunque es de noche.*

> This eternal spring is hidden
> In this living bread for our life's sake,
> > Although it is night.

> It is here to call to creatures and they
> Are filled with this water, although in darkness,
> > Because it is night.

---

163. Text in *Enchiridion Fontium Historiae Ecclesiasticae Antiquae* (New York: Herder, 1965), no. 1.

This living spring which I long for,
I see in this bread of life,
Although it is night.[164]

---

164. *Song of the soul that rejoices in knowing God through faith.* From *The Collected Works of St. John of the Cross,* translated by Kieran Kavanaugh and Otilio Rodriguez. Copyright © 1964, 1979, 1991 by Washington Province of Discalced Carmelites ICS Publications 2131 Lincoln Road, N.E. Washington, DC 20002-1199 U.S.A. www.icspublications.org

Raniero Cantalamessa is a Franciscan Capuchin Catholic priest. In 1980, Pope John Paul II appointed him Preacher to the Papal Household, a title also known as the Apostolic Preacher. In this role, he preached a weekly sermon in Advent and Lent in the presence of the Pope, the cardinals, bishops, and prelates of the Roman Curia, and the general superiors of religious orders. He also frequently speaks at international and ecumenical conferences and rallies, has been a member of the Catholic delegation for Dialogue with the Pentecostal Churches for the last ten years, and runs a weekly program on the Gospel on the first channel of Italian state television. His numerous books have been published in many languages.

BOOKS & MEDIA

The Daughters of St. Paul operate book and media centers at the following addresses. Visit, call or write the one nearest you today, or find us on the World Wide Web, www.pauline.org

CALIFORNIA

3908 Sepulveda Blvd, Culver City, CA 90230	310-397-8676
5945 Balboa Avenue, San Diego, CA 92111	858-565-9181
46 Geary Street, San Francisco, CA 94108	415-781-5180

FLORIDA

145 S.W. 107th Avenue, Miami, FL 33174	305-559-6715

HAWAII

1143 Bishop Street, Honolulu, HI 96813	808-521-2731
Neighbor Islands call:	866-521-2731

ILLINOIS

172 North Michigan Avenue, Chicago, IL 60601	312-346-4228

LOUISIANA

4403 Veterans Memorial Blvd, Metairie, LA 70006	504-887-7631

MASSACHUSETTS

885 Providence Hwy, Dedham, MA 02026	781-326-5385

MISSOURI

9804 Watson Road, St. Louis, MO 63126	314-965-3512

NEW JERSEY

561 U.S. Route 1, Wick Plaza, Edison, NJ 08817	732-572-1200

NEW YORK

150 East 52nd Street, New York, NY 10022	212-754-1110

PENNSYLVANIA

9171-A Roosevelt Blvd, Philadelphia, PA 19114	215-676-9494

SOUTH CAROLINA

243 King Street, Charleston, SC 29401	843-577-0175

TENNESSEE

4811 Poplar Avenue, Memphis, TN 38117	901-761-2987

TEXAS

114 Main Plaza, San Antonio, TX 78205	210-224-8101

VIRGINIA

1025 King Street, Alexandria, VA 22314	703-549-3806

CANADA

3022 Dufferin Street, Toronto, ON M6B 3T5	416-781-9131

¡También somos su fuente para libros,
videos y música en español!